The Arts and Critical Thinking in American Education

The Arts and Critical Thinking in American Education

Ivan Olson

Ralph A. Smith, Advisory Editor

BERGIN & GARVEY
Westport, Connecticut • London

Library of Congress Cataloging-in-Publication Data

Olson, Ivan, 1931–
     The arts and critical thinking in American education / Ivan Olson.
        p.   cm.
     Includes bibliographical references and index.
     ISBN 0–89789–694–7 (alk. paper)
     1. Aesthetics.   2. Critical thinking.   3. Creative thinking.
     4. Art—Philosophy.   I. Title.
     BH39.045   2000
     111'.85—dc21   98–30497

British Library Cataloguing in Publication Data is available.

Library of Congress Catalog Card Number: 98–30497
ISBN: 0–89789–694–7

First published in 2000

Bergin & Garvey, 88 Post Road West, Westport, CT 06881
An imprint of Greenwood Publishing Group, Inc.
www.greenwood.com

Printed in the United States of America

The paper used in this book complies with the
Permanent Paper Standard issued by the National
Information Standards Organization (Z39.48–1984).

10 9 8 7 6 5 4 3 2 1

Contents

Illustrations

Preface

Educational issues such as reform, school vouchers, and standardized testing have shared the educational spotlight in recent years. Of these three issues, reform has become the ever present one, drawing into its circle not only the other two, but also other "hot" issues such as standards, quality, curriculum development, and budget, as well as defining and investigating the processes of learning, teaching, and creativity.

As this ubiquitous reform movement continues to take shape, there appear more and more opportunities for focus and discovery within the various academic disciplines, including all the arts. These are opportunities for us to gain new insights into the learning processes, to not only better understand ourselves as creatures of thought and reflection, but also add to our understanding of the "hows and whys" of our "adventures of the mind." The arts are truly adventures of the mind, yet only a very small proportion of our society approach them as such. With that in mind, this text focuses on three approaches which hopefully will stimulate further interest and study in descriptive and experimental aesthetics as they can and should be applied to the core of our educational curricula and programs in general: (1) realization of the arts as cognitive and affective essentials in human development; (2) the necessity of a controlled and dynamic tandem of perception and cognition for meaningful experiences in the arts; and (3) how important our imaging processes are in all arts experiences.

Introduction

This text combines an amalgam of philosophical reflection with active empirical studies, as well as eighteenth- and nineteenth-century formalism. Also included are discussions of theory of illumination, retinal reception, and cognitive color theories. Many topics, diverse in themselves, have been brought together to offer a resource for discussion and investigation in the areas of learning processes, teaching, and creativity.

The text takes the reader from an overview of some of the foundational work relating to philosophy, critical thinking, aesthetic processes, "awareness," and the mind, through several chapters which will continuously define or redefine *critical thinking, creativity,* and *cultural literacy.* Chapter one will present what I believe to be a necessary philosophical overview. In it the reader will find an emphasis on the foundational work of some of the great idealist and realist thinkers as it has influenced our attitudes and approaches to arts experiences, as well as experiences in the other areas of life experiences. Chapter two emphasizes perception and cognition as an important combination, almost inseparable in the three levels of arts activities: creating, presenting, and receiving. Chapters three and four delve deeply into material which is often overlooked in arts or aesthetics issues. I am hopeful that the reader will find helpful resource material here in the discussion of the human developmental processes, art and absorption, the psyche, and defining creativity, all of this brought together under the umbrella of critical thinking. In chapter four, particularly, I present one of the least known cognitive areas of study and issues: imagery. I am convinced that this is a most important area—recent literature shows that many others now agree with me— and certainly needs and deserves continuous exploration. Chapter five returns to an overview approach, not as that found in the first chapter, but now as an attempt to relate our ideas, experiments, data, conclusions, and reflections to present day, everyday life. Chapter six offers teaching materials and approaches which might serve as meaningful supplements for teachers who are always searching for materials to use in discovery/inquiry learning sessions within or beyond their conventional class sessions. All thirteen examples rely on a focus and discovery approach that is employed to reinforce some of the concepts of various aesthetic processes within the other chapters. Particular emphasis is given to the concepts of conservation and activation within the structure of several of the examples. The appendix is offered with sincere hopes that the *Taxonomy* will serve not just as a resource of terms, definitions, and ideas, but rather, as an attempt to set out a meaningful picture, a catalyst, if you will, for increased serious study of aesthetic experience as an essential ingredient in the human mind and spirit.

1

Theoretical and Philosophical Overview

IDEALISM AND THE ARTS

If a philosophy is a system of interrelated assumptions so basic as to apply to every area of experience, then in our philosophical approach it becomes necessary first to come to an understanding of how many usable and acceptable approaches to philosophy exist in the modern world, and how long they have existed. With all the "isms" and vogue philosophies that have appeared in our media and literature during the past century, it becomes necessary in any philosophical endeavor to sort out the ways in which we experience and understand.

Most scholars would agree that over the years there have been four basic philosophies: naturalism, idealism, realism, and pragmatism. Two of these, idealism and realism, include much concern for aesthetic experience and understanding. This is not to say that the other two philosophies do not include some philosophy of art, or aesthetics. They certainly do. However, idealism and realism have been represented by thinking that allows for unlimited consideration of aesthetics; that is, perception of, and reflection of, life experiences or phenomena.

Idealism, together with the more modern branch of philosophy, realism, offers more connections with the arts and aesthetic process than probably any of the other areas of philosophy. Also, the age of Plato and Socrates, with its beginnings of Western idealism, would be succeeded by a Hebrew-Christian era of more than fifteen centuries that would influence and shape the worldview, East or West, in terms of aesthetics as well as religious, social, economic, and scientific outlook. As this was a period for recognized intellectual leadership by clergy, it was most significant that philosophy was sympathetic toward religion. Such idealists as St. Augustine in the fifth century and St. Thomas Aquinas in the thirteenth century transposed some aspects of religious faith and experience into intellectual terms. In the modern world, as Christians (Catholic or Protestant) or non-Christians, we can remind ourselves that the works of Augustine and Aquinas became the generators of the "criterion of truth" for the Catholic Church (Butler, 293). Built upon ancient Greek, Egyptian, and Arabian traditions of inquiry, reflection, and revelation, the cathedrals also became havens of thought based on centuries of idealism, Platonic and Aristotelian logic, and, in time, the materialism of naturalist thought, as well.

As we turn our attention to philosophic thought after 1500, it might serve us well to focus on four idealists, Descartes, Kant, Hegel, and Schopenhauer, the first two also considered to be realists.

Rene Descartes (1596–1650), author of the universally known statement, "I think, therefore I am," expounded on the significance of the self. He accepted the reality of the self as beyond doubt; it is empirical, firsthand, immediate experience. Descartes emphasized that any other experience is once-removed; the self is the necessary starting point in thought. As a prime mover of ideas for the Age of Reason and the Enlightenment, he spoke of the idea of the perfect being and the existence of God. His belief in natural law and universal order exerted great influence on moral, social, and scientific issues, fostering a logical and scientific approach that was injected also into theories and criticism in music and the visual arts.

For a full century, from 1650 to 1750, or from the end of Descartes's life until Immanuel Kant's adulthood, three scholars carried on the idealist tradition and, like Descartes, also developed ideas in the newer philosophy of realism. Baruch Spinoza, Gottfried Leibniz, and George Berkeley all contributed a kind of metaphysics that forecast late-nineteenth-century physics and aesthetics with strong differentiation drawn between theory and empiricism. All three, particularly Spinoza, carry over to a certain extent the idea of God as a thinking being. The atomistic concept of Leibniz relied on an image—not very far removed from twentieth-century physics—of the universe comprised of particles of energy he chose to label as "monads," and which existed at three levels: basic—perceptual with life continuity; higher order—soul; highest order—spirit. All three scholars accepted such a hierarchy as the main difference between humans and "lower" animals, in which three levels of life in the Leibniz configuration play out as follows: sense—sensations, sense—intelligence, reason—understanding.

George Berkeley (1685–1753), in age the last of this triad of philosophers, probably profited by the new directions found in writings of the seventeenth and eighteenth centuries, many of which expounded on human understanding and set intellectual precedents that worked continuously toward the development of studies in medicine, sociology, psychology, experimental physical sciences, and aesthetics, among which were the discoveries in physics by Isaac Newton and the rediscovery of works on experimental interpretation of nature by Francis Bacon.

We can treat Berkeley's work as the final pre-Kantian effort in idealism. His treatise, "The Principles of Human Knowledge," remains one of the major treatises in philosophy. In consideration of the purpose and bias of this text—to give special emphasis to aesthetic experience and the process of critical thinking—it should not be out of order to consider Berkeley as the "beginning" of the culmination of the centuries-old tradition of Hebrew-Christian Idealism, with the final culmination of this movement to be found in the works of Kant, Hegel, and Schopenhauer.

To Berkeley, "spirit" represents active being. Such being has two domains: external and internal. The external to Berkeley is basic perception, senses; the internal is reason and understanding.

By Spirit, Berkeley means a simple undivided active being whose two principal activities are creating and perceiving. Perceiving is the understanding aspect of spirit, and creating is the willing or volitional aspect. This metaphysical theory is that reality is through and through what we experience it to be within ourselves, i.e., mentality. (Butler, 150)

This concept remains essential even for modern thought in understanding critical thinking, creativity, memory, and imagery; it will appear frequently in chapters three, four, and five. Often Berkeley invokes concepts in aesthetic experience that have extended well into the twentieth century. One such concept is that the creative mind is never neutral, but is strongly for or against (Butler, 149–150). The epitome of his most subjective, idealist side is his doctrine that "the world, as we perceive it, depends on our perceiving consciousness for its existence in the form in which we know it. 'To be is to be perceived'" (Butler, 151). Some of Berkeley's 250-year-old concepts extend to the twentieth century, and will be mentioned again (chapter four) in discussion of questions about images and image generation in arts experiences.

David Hume (1711–1776) is included in this text not because he is generally considered one of the important philosophers of the eighteenth century, but because he prepared a brilliant analysis of the knowledge and learning process. Entitled "A Treatise of Human Nature," this analysis was not considered very significant by the literati of his time—in fact, it was considered heretical by many. However, Will Durant, among many modern scholars, considers it "one of the classics and marvels of modern philosophy" (Durant, 195). In the treatise, Hume speaks of ideas, their origin, composition, connection, and abstraction. In Part One, he separates perceptions of the human mind into two categories: impressions and ideas. "The difference betwixt these consists in the degrees of force and liveliness with which they strike upon the mind, and make their way into our thought or consciousness" (Hume, 9). He considered impressions as more of what we might consider today as affect: emotions, passions, sensations; and considered ideas as what we would think of as cognition: images in thinking and reasoning. We are still employing those categories today in most discussions of thought process, and although we might not agree to the letter on some of Hume's later radical skepticism, we find such disagreement probably to be more semantic than substantive.

Hume's skepticism did not allow him to distinguish "mind" from brain. He maintained that we know the mind only as we know matter; we perceive that matter. In artistic tasks or experiences, however, we have "internal voices," we perceive internally. However, we can agree with Hume that the mind is not a substance.

But let's take a closer look! For the creative writer, painter, composer, or choreographer, the aesthetic detail becomes simple. All Hume has said is that the mind is not an organ that has ideas; it is rather "an abstract name for series of separate ideas, feelings, and memories" (Durant, 195). However, in modern aesthetics, with the inherited benefit of centuries of disputations, we have generally accepted the concept of various degrees of knowledge, memory, creativity, and feeling all existing within us, available for different degrees of "renewable existence" upon demand without the total need of external perception, just as we have the constant ability also to experience awareness through any degree of external perception and processing.

This two-hundred-years war of the philosophers from Descartes to Kant went far beyond aesthetics or philosophy of art; it involved the two opposing concepts: (1) no matter exists, it's only in the mind, versus (2) we know the mind only as we know matter. Outside the arts, this issue remained intense as it involved the concepts of soul and natural law.

The arts are the only cumulative area of human experience in which the soul and natural law are not a problem. Yet the world of the arts, its sociology, its psychology, its creativity, all are intensely involved in debate, rebellion, redemption, and revelation which touch upon a central point: human intelligence and the image. Throughout this text we will constantly relate imaging to the learning process, as well as to memory and creativity.

Immanuel Kant (1724–1804), one of the greatest philosophers of any period, devoted much of his effort toward a precise analysis of the knowledge process. Kant maintained that humans relate all sensations by locating them in space and time. "We see objects which are units in themselves as external to us, and as related to other objects in an orderly way" (Butler, 153). Twentieth-century aesthetic thought certainly reflects some of the Kantian concern for form. This emphasis on form or structure pervaded much of Kant's writing. To him, form represented a necessary ingredient in any recipe for logic and awareness. This form includes an array of specific characteristics, among them unity, variety, and balance. Kant believed that when one is aware of such form as unity or balance, he is at a level of perception higher than mere sensation (sight, sound, touch, taste, smell).

Although he did not have the benefit of data from neurological discoveries and lab experiences as we do today, Kant was aware that the human organism receives sensations with its sensory organs continuously and involuntarily with little or no thought about them, even though they definitely impress the organism. For example, a gallery visitor, while enjoying the many paintings and sculptures on display, might be spending an inordinate amount of time in front of a particular painting. Portions of the floor have been cleaned with a strong lemon-like compound; diffused sunlight is pouring through the skylight panels; other visitors in that room are conversing politely, but audibly; the visitor's right foot has begun to hurt a bit due to excessive rubbing by the heel of the shoe. He is immersed mentally in the painting confronting him, and it seems as if the only thing he is aware of at that moment is the beautiful brushwork and blending of different greens broken by gray shadows in a mid-nineteenth-century landscape. He walks away from the painting and realizes that his foot hurts, sniffs a few times of the aromatic lemony air, and suddenly becomes aware of the brightness of the pervasive sunlight in the room and how it accents the forms, outlines, and space. His sensory receptors had indeed received images; they were all busy at times. Thus, as Kant had thought it out, the visitor's external world was represented to him by means of his various senses. At a given moment, he had many different sensations that were not heeded until he stopped to give them attention. This stopping to give attention to other things allows the visitor to become more aware of the natural light, among other things, which his brain will be able to call up and represent. It will also be capable of recalling and then representing. Thus, they are representations, not presentations. We might think of them as copies of what is "out there" in the physical world (Butler, 152).

G. W. Friedrich Hegel (1770–1831) produced philosophical arguments that remain essential in twentieth-century aesthetic thought. The idea of the "gestalt" can be attributed as much to Hegel as to any other scholar, scientist, or philosopher of the nineteenth century. Such a concept, dealing with wholeness of objects or experiences as they are related in some kind of totality, can be seen "in a motif running throughout Hegel's philosophy which is to the effect that parts must always be viewed in relation to the whole, never in isolation" (Butler, 159).

Hegel's patterns of dialectic have contributed to the shaping of modern aesthetics and critical thinking. One of his most prominent methods was the triad of thesis—antithesis—synthesis, in which thesis relates to Idea, antithesis to Nature, and synthesis to Mind or Spirit. The first and second components are contradictory, and the third forms a unity out of the positive elements of the first two.

We should not underestimate the importance of Hegel's concern for form and its implications. From 1750 to 1875 all of the arts were under the stylistic spell of formalism, represented in the French architecture of Gabriel, the sculpture of Houdon, the paintings of David, and the music of Haydn and Mozart. Formal logic was so well-nested in the arts and aesthetic outlook of the Classic-Romantic periods that this formalism thrived in the output of hundreds of great painters, composers, sculptors, and architects into the twentieth century. The importance of formal logic in the arts will continue to be a focal point later on in this text.

Arthur Schopenhauer (1788–1860) during his lifetime never quite achieved the status of successor to Kant and rival to Hegel. However, by the end of the nineteenth century, and since then, his influence has increased. His philosophical approaches have not waned; rather, they exhibit a broader popularity than ever, particularly in the area of aesthetics. His writings greatly influenced Freud and Nietzsche.

Kant and Schopenhauer, both idealists, were both creative minds, ahead of their times; yet they were fully aware of, and able to use, thoughts of the past, for example, the Platonic Idea (an idea represented by a particular object). "Arthur Schopenhauer has been to aesthetics what Kant has been to ethics, a great creator in the idealist tradition" (Butler, 212).

Although Schopenhauer, in his statement that art was "the flower of life," might have sounded a bit sentimental, we are assured that he was relating mostly to aesthetic values. Because he thought many problems of the world arose because of individuality, he believed that one must understand fully what it means to be human, an individual, living a recurring cycle of desire, struggle, and striving accompanied by pain and temporary satisfaction, which would be followed by satiation and boredom. The cycle would then repeat. Because of this outlook, Schopenhauer was labeled by many of his contemporaries as a pessimist. However, one could hardly think of him as a hard-core pessimist in terms of his aesthetics.

A closer look at Schopenhauer's aesthetics might add to our understanding of the idealist philosophy in a broader sense. Below are included his more powerful and influential ideas which yet abound in modern and postmodern writings:

1. The more individuals can rise above the restraints of individuality, the more they can be released from a pattern of desire—struggle—striving—satiation—boredom.

2. Art is a level of experience to which humans can rise and which promises momentary release from their own individuality.

3. Two values that we might possess by entering into any kind of aesthetic experience, be it creating, presenting, or receiving, are a knowledge of the object, and a momentary will-less existence, totally immersed in attention to the art object.

When we "lose" ourselves in a painting, we become totally objective, we become the will-less receptors of an image. According to Schopenhauer, when we listen to music we are transcending forms of Nature. Music is the highest of the arts, as it is not so much concerned with objects and ideas. Rather, it is concerned with Will, the essence of the object. "Music is transfigured Nature and could exist to an extent without the natural order" (Butler, 213).

As insightful as it is, Schopenhauer's approach to aesthetics does have its weaknesses, those evident mainly within the concepts of form, particularly in music, in which he states that "music is an expression of will which is free both of the Ideas and the principle of individual forms" (Butler, 213). Even if we agree that this weakness does exist, we can most surely excuse him for it, as he had almost none of the studies of which we can take advantage: treatises and experimental data in modern neurosciences, psychology, audiology, acoustics, and other cognitive sciences, vast arrays of material which give us much to think about, and on which to build future studies that will help us to better understand such things as brain, mind, image, inner pictures, and voices.

REALISM IN THE ARTS

As mentioned earlier, idealism and realism are accepted as philosophies that for many centuries have allowed for the consideration and contemplation of aesthetic experiences. Thus far, I have attempted to emphasize that idealism, with its longer history, has furnished the "cradle" for western aesthetic thought. It remains to very generally compare realism with idealism in order to gain some perspective of the continuation of this aesthetic concern through the ages.

Idealism promotes the concept that reality exists only in the mind; therefore, phenomena and objects are representations of the mind. In contrast, realism takes on the perspective of life-experiences and phenomena that center on unembellished renderings of natural forms. A most important tenet of realism is that universals exist independently of the human mind. This becomes important to us because it points toward aesthetic phenomena always derived from metaphysical entities that themselves are constants. They are unchanged and repeatable in character, even when existing among series of changes. In my opinion, it is this constancy that underpins any cultural movement toward any moments of artistic expression and consensus.

Realism goes all the way back to Aristotle; it is then represented by a line of philosophers who in their ruminations on aesthetic phenomena might be considered more as idealists than anything else: Aquinas (1225–1274), Descartes (1596–1650), Spinoza (1632–1677), Locke (1632–1704), Kant (1724–1804), James (1842–1910), as well as twentieth-century neorealist W. P. Montague and critical realist George Santayana.

We think of realism as a more recent philosophic movement than idealism. From the sixteenth century to late nineteenth century, realist thought existed marginally, with many of its contributions also espousing idealist ideas. Among many different varieties of realism the common emphasis was the rejection of the idealist *Theory of Knowledge*. Even though a chaotic mixture of difference and agreement existed between the two groups and between individuals in various areas of reasoning, those developments appear, in themselves, to be of little consequence to the arts. Aesthetics, or the philosophy of art, draws from both the idealist and realist approaches.

William James represents the beginning of the modern realist movement in America. Such a position probably evolved out of his reaction against idealism. Although we hold for James a most lofty place as pragmatist, any influence he has had on the arts has been as a realist. Considered by many as the father of both American philosophy movements, realism and pragmatism, James had a background as close to perfect for the task as one could ever hope to find: serious art study in Paris and America as a teenager; then college study in biology, medicine, psychology, and philosophy; then his long teaching career at Harvard in physiology, psychology, and philosophy, in that order.

James argued that consciousness is a nonentity with no existence of its own. It is a function of experience. He stated that knowing is a simple relation with objects that are presented, not represented. Consciousness and experience are collective terms. As a pluralist, he reacted against the speculative aspects of the idealists when he emphasized that all kinds of qualities, substances, shapes, and essences exist in time and space (James, 1948). Experience is a kind of relation—we might better think of it in the arts as a kind of condition—with which we build our knowledge base.

Modern Realism

Of the several neorealists, W. P. Montague shared in their scientific spirit and their position in refuting the idealist principle that knowledge of an object brings about changes in that particular object. Most helpful in informing us about the neorealist attitude toward the nature of aesthetic experience are Montague's statements that (1) aesthetic value is the enjoyment that results from experiences in which cognition and feeling blend; (2) beauty is not necessarily in just the perception itself, but in experiences with subtle associations; and (3) "beauty" has been too narrowly conceived; there are other kinds of aesthetic value in addition to beauty (Montague, 1925: 128).

George Santayana, an American philosopher of Spanish birth, was one of the critical realists who rejected the tenet of the neorealists that objects are directly presented to consciousness. Instead, the critical realists stated that objects are not presented, but represented. Sound familiar? How about the old idealists? Yes! Not only were American philosophers becoming very specific, they were also becoming, like their French, German, and British colleagues, very pedantic and very prolix. Nevertheless, during the first half of the twentieth century, American philosophers had gained an important position in the world of letters. It is not by accident that this all-too-brief over-view ends with the ideas of George Santayana. The work of Santayana represents a compatible philosophical base for aesthetic principles of our time, principles that are dynamic and credible. Santayana's aesthetic did not omit the idea of essence as a quality that represents to us objects of the world through our powers of perception. He viewed the mind in a physical con-text, yet emphasized its mental, rational, and imaginative vision of qualities or characteristics of objects, feelings, conditions, and relationships. The short summary below represents three distinct and prominent ideas coming from over two thousand years of philosophy. This summary might help to lead us into the subject area of "perceptual style and the arts" in the following chapter.

- The mind is like a mirror receiving images from the physical world. (Comenius)
- Our minds are like blank pages at birth upon which the world proceeds to write its impression. (Locke)
- Consciousness is an awareness of experience, and experience is a medium in which objects and organisms are related. (James)

EIGHT TERMS IN NEED OF SPECIAL ATTENTION

The use of the terms included below is somewhat inconsistent by dic-tionary standards, and that is the reason why I choose to focus on them for a moment. For decades, many such terms have been acquired from our daily working vocabulary, and find their way into new dimensions of more abstract and conceptual meaning. Throughout the text I work to define and redefine some of them. The very existence of each of these terms is the result of var-ied acceptance, interpretation, and use. They are gray area concepts to many intelligent individuals because of the variances; yet, they are critical in any serious discussion that might link the aesthetic process to critical thinking, this being particularly true in any activity of inquiry or discovery or focus which is built on the many centuries of idealist and realist thinking.

Acculturation—the process of adopting social patterns of a different group. The defi-nition implies linear process.

Cognition—originality of thought, finding new ways to solve problems; using what might be novel, fitting, of good qualities, to counterbalance the repetitious and ba-nal; thinking.

Critical thinking—a disciplined process of analyzing, synthesizing, or evaluating in-formation resulting from observation, reasoning, or reflection, based upon intellec-tual values that apply to all areas of human experience.

Cultural literacy—one of the more contentious terms, it is used in both its sociologi-cal and aesthetic contexts herein. Cultural literacy denotes an understanding and aware-ness of the sum total of ways of living developed over the years by a group of human beings. This awareness carries over from one generation to another, in which there is recognition of persons or societies by hallmarks that reflect their manners, letters, arts, and general civil and humane behavior.

Eidetic—pertaining to visual imagery and, to some extent, to auditory imagery retained in short-term or long-term memory that is readily reproducible, sometimes with great accuracy. There will be no reference to "photographic memory," as the existence of such phenomena has never been proven or even logically inferred.

Imagery—an important term in any study of thinking, memory, learning, or responding. Our minds cannot move from one simple thought to another without reliance upon some kind of imaging process.

Perception—we will deal with this term as both empirical and conceptual in meaning: gathering of information by any or all of the senses, immediate or intuitive recognition, and sometimes denoting precognitive modes leading to cognitive modes in the brain.

Perceptual style—along the way we will employ this term very specifically as field dependent/independent modes of thinking or global/specific.

I have laid out several conceptual points as issues that continue the discussion of the two major philosophical schools of thought, idealism and realism, as they specifically relate to American arts education, critical thinking, and aesthetic values.

THE AMERICAN ATTITUDE

As we define and explore such things as cultural literacy, imagery, and perceptual style in seeking our overall perspective of aesthetic experiences and attitudes in the United States and the rest of the world, we will continue to build upon many of the idealistic and realistic concepts which have for two millennia served as irrevocable touchstones.

The following are seven issues for us to consider in arriving at a clearer picture of the "American attitude" and expectations for the arts in education, and how we think about them. I hope that the reader will find the topics and related issues herein to be logical starting points for production of significant questions worthy of study.

1. Intrinsic values. As we come to the end of the twentieth century, less and less is mentioned in public of these kinds of values. Is a society wherein the main features of noteworthiness seem to be affluence, financial power, political power, and public exposure at serious risk of decline? Are America's cultural efforts, its cultural literacy, in decline?

2. Concrete truths do exist: universal truths exist; individuality remains the locus and measure of value. However, the "anything goes, anything acceptable as good" philosophy surrounds us.

3. Refinement of perception is a necessity for our civilization. It should be important to all of us that we become as aware of the world around us as we

possibly can. Our pleasure can be measured, to a certain degree, by the quality of our awareness.

4. "Knowledge gathering" should be an objective in our daily lives.

5. A type of neorealism will probably exist in the visual arts throughout all eras of civilization. As humans, we have a strong need for the representational, no matter how appealing and entertaining fantasy might be. To be sure, another one of our "isms," dedicated to realism, is verism, which is the theory that a strong representation of truth and reality is necessary for art, drama, and literature. The interesting corollary of this is that because of the need for verism, the ugly and grotesque must be included with the beautiful and well-organized.

6. The concept of reconstructionism remains a troublesome one for all except those who oppose the philosophies of realism and idealism. These are the people who are constantly ready to remake society according to what they believe it should be. Reconstruction feeds on an overriding concern for contemporary cultural problems. This approach becomes problematic for the arts, as it begins to reframe the arts and arts education. Visual arts, music, dance, and poetry all take on the burden of propagandizing one thing or another.

7. Relativism deals first and foremost with social context. In fact, the social context—"social-historical relativity" as Arthur Child (1944) calls it—is the *raison d'etre* for relativism. In any application of the arts, Child claims, there must be an acknowledgment of the social-historical relativity of aesthetic value. If we discuss aesthetics in terms of "felt qualities," we must approach the phenomena by differentiating between the aesthetic experience and the aesthetic value. Child made the cogent observation that one does not necessarily have to value highly an art object or experience in order to enjoy it at any moment. I believe that this implies that the highest of aesthetic phenomena is that which is both enjoyed to the maximum and is considered to be of inestimably high value. The significance of Child's presentments can be centered on one statement: "Social-historical relativism mediates, in the theory of the esthetic judgment, between the polar errors of absolute universalism and absolute relativism" (Child, 3–22).

We know that individuals, young or old, cannot obtain a desired aesthetic response simply by willing to have it. Mentors should keep in mind the premise that two factors always exist in aesthetic experience, objective ground and aesthetic subjectivity, both of which are tempered by abstraction and social subjectivity. Teachers of the arts must consider what to, how to, and why inculcate culture attitudes. We should better inculcate attitudes such as the desire to seek understanding and appreciation of great art works and their powerful intrinsic values. No one, young or old, well-schooled or unschooled, has ever been hurt by such inculcation. Only when such things as opportunism and social dogma or political power of some kind is in the larger context can it be negative, and then it becomes a darker side of our existence, and it is no longer art. Political context and other irrelevant biases take away from the essence of the art process; it detracts from a greater general awareness of the miracle of the human spirit. Not to be given the chance to become aware of the human brilliance, intellectual nuances, and spirit in a Mozart piano concerto, for example, would indeed be a shame.

As we consider the basic and vital function of human perception in the next chapter, please keep in mind that our conceptual burden is heavy. We will be bringing together such concepts as visual and auditory perception, perception as determined by the immediate environment, psychophysiological reception of art's characteristics and properties, and various other concepts that become important to us in any inquiry about creativity, critical thinking, and aesthetic awareness. In the following chapters, much of the text will reflect a determination not to be entrapped by either of the extreme positions of absolute relativism or absolute universals. Unlike Child, however, I cannot subscribe to a concept of social historical relativism existing as a mediating factor between the two poles of aesthetic judgment, as I believe that such a concept actually works in opposition to any application of universals. Many great scholars, scientists, and inventors of the twentieth century, Bertrand Russell, Loren Eisely, Walter Gropius, and Fred Hoyle, to name a few, have girded some of their more significant ideas with universals, yet have ignored such universals in much of their dialectic efforts. All four believe that civilization as we know it is first and foremost part of an expanding mental universe. Yet, they reflect the general temper of modern society in their emphasis on such concepts as individualism versus conformity, art as creative activity, concepts of relativity, and relationship of perception to value. If we truly are part of an expanding mental universe, then we must recognize the existence of essential universals, which often serve as foundations for continuous building.

My intentions are not to offer any influences toward certain philosophic positions on universals, but rather to simply emphasize—as I will in several different sections of this text—how important the consideration of the topic is in any discussion of aesthetics as part of the mental universe.

2

Perceptual Style

It might be of value at this point to give some attention to the dichotomous quality of "perception." In some literature the term might be used to denote a generalization or some kind of intellectual or logical insight or some special sensory awareness—for example, awareness of a pleasant effect resulting from the interplay of light and soft shadows produced by a setting sun on a tropical island. Or, it might refer specifically and technically to perception as a process of our neurophysiology, our sensing mechanisms such as visual processing in which the signals are running from the retina to the visual cortex, giving the brain the information necessary for the process.

If we can accept and use this dichotomous concept of perception, we should find it to be a logical task to consider two of the five sensory modalities (sight, sound, touch, taste, and smell) of perceptual process, the visual and the aural, to the extent that we can form valid generalizations in order to relate them to both the physical (empirical) and metaphysical (conceptual or abstract) approaches to understanding. This might promote better understanding of principles of critical thinking, creativity, external and internal thinking processes, memory, and last, but certainly not least, two areas that I think of as special modalities: the intuitive and the kinesthetic, which in some way touch upon all the others.

FROM PERCEPTION TO COGNITION

For the time being, let us simplify the true differences between perception and cognition. Most basic, and most important, the process of perception is autonomic (involuntary). When we see or hear something, the phenomenon is, simply, there. We experience it; it happened. We have little or no option for it not to happen. However, cognition is voluntary; it deals with ideas and concepts. It processes all kinds of problem-solving insights and understandings, associations, and relationships that are based upon facts. Thus, when a painter stands at her canvas, carefully studying a still-life arrangement nearby, her autonomic neural system is passing on visual information to the brain; and this perceptual process enables the cognitive activity to begin, and as it does, the cognition could amount to any degree of nervous system response, even as much as a continuous stream of ideas, concepts, solutions, objectives, and anticipations.

We should not downplay the role of perception, as it becomes an integral part of the learning process to the extent that the degree of quality and accuracy of our sensory impressions will weigh heavily on quality of information to be processed by the brain. For those close to the arts, the descriptor phrase "from perception to cognition" is bursting with recondite meaning, as in any of the three aesthetic modes—creating, performing/displaying, or receiving—the nerve cells are communicating chemically, informing by electric signals. Those of us close to the arts, but not close to neurophysiology, might take into account the awesome phenomenon that is the human brain. Before any kind of scenario of an aesthetic experience would be completed for one person, interactions would occur among a large portion of the nearly one trillion nerve cells in a human brain. And, each of those cells (neurons) can make as many as ten thousand connections with other cells. A single neuron might possess an enormous number of axons (processes), and some of those axons, transmitting electrical impulses, might extend several feet in length (Dowling, 1992: 49–125). Thus, we have a neuronal structure in which the majority of interactions in the brain occur among the various long processes or axons. Add to all this the fact that the retina in the eye has five different types of neurons and photoreceptors, the cerebellum five types, and the cerebral cortex two types. Certain cells have specific jobs; they are identified as association neurons, of which two kinds both send and receive synaptic contacts. Synapses, as functional contacts between neurons, are the modifiers of memory and learning.

Visual Perception

Initial stages of visual processing. In the beginning of the process only photoreceptors respond directly to a light stimulus. All other cells are activated by signals that begin with rod and cone cells.

Retinal processing. A binary system, the retina maintains a division of visual information in which some neurons (on-center cells) give light increments to the brain, and other neurons (off-center cells) give light decrements.

Light distribution. Other cells in the retina respond to differentiate and accommodate three categories of illumination: central illumination, surround illumination, and diffuse illumination.

Although our concern with visual processing has taken us only to the initial activity of the retina, we already are able to deal with such a concept as color intensity and how the retina handles it. Those cells that respond to surround illumination dramatically affect our perception of color intensity or depth. Such responding neurons present to us a system in which "our judgment of intensity depends on surrounding illumination" (Dowling, 1992: 317). Even before scholars and neuroscientists were proving theories relating to field, ground effects, intensity, and the like, artists were painting landscapes and still life forms with understanding of the general concept that in any real visual impression the value (brightness) of the hues and the saturation level in a painting are very much relative. A stationary object in a scene might on a sunny day appear brilliant, yet on a cloudy day seem moderately light and faded in comparison. This relative change in value would probably be exhibited by other objects in the scene as well.

As was mentioned earlier, the retina's binary system of illumination is what one might think of as a super-adaptor, an accommodator. Central illumination occurs when the natural (real) scene is such that a particular object or area is brighter and/or lighter than the rest of the scene around it. Surround illumination constitutes a situation where the field or ground around the object or area in focus is brighter and/or lighter. Finally, diffuse illumination occurs when the entire field or ground seems to present what might be called a more homogeneous ground, one in which the value is consistent throughout the scene. Two Monet works are noted below as examples of the surround and diffuse conditions. An example of central illumination is Rembrandt's *Portrait of a Young Man* (1655), in which the face and neck-chain are overwhelmingly the focus against a relatively dark and saturated background and foreground.

Claude Monet (1840–1926), who is considered to be the earliest and most important of the Impressionist painters, viewed painting as an optical experience. Convinced that the eye does not seek out minute details in objects, he purposely omitted details that were not fundamental to the recognition of light, color, and general configuration.

In his paintings, Monet emphasized the change of scenes brought about by different weather and lighting conditions. As a result, many of his paintings are atmospheric, with traditional outlining or highlighting deemphasized. Such an approach produced paintings which relied more on lighter shades of color, and in which the forms, although not distorted, were often made more obscure. (Olson, 1981: 160)

Examples of paintings abound in which light distribution becomes an important artistic or aesthetic factor. In the relatively short period of 1875 to 1925, one can find such "crowning" examples as Monet's *Field of Poppies*, in which the diffuse illumination is such a strong factor that many viewers of the painting are hardly aware of a second human figure in the painting. For an example of surround illumination, Monet's *The River* presents an impelling use of light and color (see Illustration 2.1). The hues of pink, blue, and light olive-green meet in a background of sky and cliffs to give way to the grayish ecru color values of rooftops. In the foreground the chalky blue of the river is partially masked by the olive-green, pink, and ecru reflections. The drenching sunlight is broken at the left side of the scene by two large shade trees, under which sits a youth. The brightness of the jacket, a pillow, and the brimmed hat almost match the brilliance of a building's reflection in the water, visible under and beyond the dark and thick shaded side of the tree.

Those who view this painting for the first time will probably think of the tree as much darker than it really is. However, no black is there, only green, and some of that is not that dark a value. On the other side of the spectrum, because of the tree and the shadows on the near bank, we can think of the rest of the scene as indeed in "drenching sunlight," including a "brilliant" reflection. Our visual process gives us that information. However, if Monet had replaced the tree with a more transparent and brilliant object, we would then have been able to observe that the relatively sunlight-drenched scene was indeed rather chalky and saturated. Light distribution is an important factor.

Auditory Perception

When describing auditory perception relative to aesthetics and the arts, cognition must also be included very early in the process. Although perception and cognition have already been separately defined in this chapter, with auditory events the boundary between the two modes becomes less clear, raising questions of if, where, when, and why they overlap.

It seems clear in tracing the perceptual processes that the trail for visual arts leads from retina to cortex, and for music it leads from cochlea to cortex. When we emphasize cognition in the next chapter the term "event perception" will appear occasionally. As a condition descriptor found frequently in neurological and psychophysiological literature, it deals with this melding of perception and cognition. In event perception there seems to be no clear line between perception and memory, as both can be extended in time. Is memory physiological or mental? Does it consist of neural connections or engrams (traces or durable marks left by a stimulus upon protoplasm)? Can memory at any moment be considered an event? These are questions that humans might continue to ask for ages and ages. Bartlett (1984) considers this issue with respect to musical perception, cognition, and memory as he states that we gather invariant information and it becomes memory. He indicates that the current research literature has established a "psychological reality of tonal structures." He and numerous other scholars have claimed va-

Ill. 2.1
Au Bord de L'Eau, Bennecourt (The River) (1868)

Claude Monet, French, 1840–1926, On the Bank of the Seine, Bennecourt (Au bord l'eau, Bennecourt), oil on canvas, 1868, 81.5 x 100.7 cm, Mr. and Mrs. Potter Palmer Collection, 1922.427. Photograph © 1997, The Art Institute of Chicago. All Rights Reserved.

lidity for that statement and three others that will all reappear in chapters three, four, and five in a variety of contexts.

1. Perception of a melody is a coherent event.

2. Melodies by virtue of their transposability are prototypical examples of wholes that are different from the sum of their parts.

3. Melodies allow for the extraction of invariants, which contribute to their coherence. This third point will undergo more thorough scrutiny later, when we apply it to specific forms, theme and variations and jazz improvisation.

If these three statements are valid, we can then consider melodies as auditory events. They are perceived as entities rather than as some kind of note grouping or sequence.

FIELD DEPENDENCE / INDEPENDENCE

Our concern for the determination of perceptual style through observation of subjects applies to both their perceptual and intellectual (cognitive) activities. Many of the instruments employed to study perceptual and cognitive style deal mainly with behavior and personality, such as the *Group Embedded Figures Test* (Witkin, et al., 1971). Use of the *Group Embedded Figures Test* (GEFT) is propitious, as the test's rationale and its construction are such that it is easily adapted to human assessment that does not have to be limited to psychopathology involving extreme dimensions of field dependence/independence. Studies employing the GEFT have demonstrated some "evidence of a higher prevalence of psychopathology at both extremes of the field dependence-independence dimension than in the middle range" (Witkin, et al., 1954). Clearly, our concerns within the study of cognitive style are those elements that relate only to creativity, imagination, and critical thinking—not to any pathology.

Study of Perceptual Styles in Music Listening

In an ongoing study (reviewed in detail in chapter four) begun in 1996, "Cognitive Events Referenced to Stimuli Produced by Specific Music Listening Experiences," I presented data that displayed a modest correlation between field independence and the ability to carry out certain music listening tasks that involved higher order cognitive exercises including memory. Terminology included three applicable definitions:

1. *Cognition*—those mental processes which include attention via perception, memory, analysis, synthesis; those activities involved in learning and creativity.

2. *Field dependence*—perceptual style in which the subject's perception is strongly

dominated by the overall organization of the surrounding field, and parts of the field are experienced as "fused" (Witkin, et al., 1971).

3. *Field independence*—perceptual style in which parts of the field are experienced as discrete from organized ground (Witkin, et al.,1971).

These three terms, among others, will persist as descriptors vital to any concept of the fusion of perception and cognition.

Over the past several decades the increased emphasis on cognitive processes in music listening as well as performance and composing has led some psychologists and music researchers to attach much more significance to the musical experience as an important part of human perception and learning.

The study of eidetic imagery as aesthetic function and phenomenon, as part of the area of critical thinking, finds its way to the arts through both psychology and philosophy. Current research and related literature, until recently, emphasized eidetic imagery as not generally related to memory ability itself; not "photographic memory," but an isolated curiosity.

Connections. If we approach eidetic imagery as both a critical thinking process and a creative process, we can with some assurance relate it to cognitive effects of certain listening experiences. A major objective of the study was to investigate the possible role that perceptual style might play in the processes of eidetic-like imagery related to musical sound stimuli.

Results. In certain tasks the subjects' perceptual style was dissimilar, and their success with the listening tasks was also dissimilar, as were the correlations between them. Evidence was obtained to support the hypothesis that the "quality" of perception was not necessarily the "style" of perception.

PERCEPTION AND THE ARTS

We have earlier in this text presumed perception to be a phenomenal process by which we obtain firsthand information from our environment. Perception involves response processes as well: selection and discrimination. In the United States during the first half of the century, perception was often considered to lie somewhere between reality and imagination, with little evidence to be found in aesthetic studies of specific attention given to either the physiological process between the retina or eardrum/cochlea and the brain, or to associations or images.

John Dewey, in "Art as Experience," spoke of aesthetic perception as including necessary energy to plunge into the subject matter and then "steep ourselves in it" (Rader, 1934: 84). Then, much in accord with the empiricists' aesthetic direction of the times in the United States, Dewey spoke strongly against the earlier nativist approach which expounded the notion that ideas and concepts of space, form, and things were innate and God given. He endorsed the empiricist idea that "knowledge arises from experience alone;

and that experience comes only by way of the senses" (quoted in Gibson, 1969: 69).

European and North American thought from the turn of the century was greatly changed or influenced in many areas by the majority acceptance of the concept of evolution. The long-reaching effect of such acceptance was a shift of transmuting proportions, bringing the nativists' structure of innate ideas and mental forms and empiricists' dynamic conditions of laws of association and experience (Warren, 118).

A Psychological Platform for Aesthetic Thought

Even though very few child psychologists in the United States were very interested in perceptual development at the beginning of the century, the subject was nevertheless given some attention, if for no other reason than that the area of child psychology, in general, was drawing increasing time, interest, and emphasis around the nation. After 1900 the supposition grew that sensory impression from the different modalities (sight, hearing, touch, taste, and smell) are additive and can become part of a total picture, idea, or image. By 1930, researchers such as Arnold Gesell had created some interest and concern in the child's sensory development, particularly that of vision, developing perceptual skills by increments (Gesell, 1934, 1949).

For the first half of the century, the arts in America profited by trends, interests, and policies in education and psychology. With a careful eye on European models, American educators were beginning to fashion their original designs for learning and achievement. During this time the two movements that then made up the fabric of American public education, behaviorism and cognitivism, each with its highly esteemed leaders, scholars, and followers, found themselves in the midst of steady financial, academic, and political support for public schools that was to continue until around mid-century.

During the period from 1900 to 1940 three important figures in education emerged as leaders of the behaviorist movement, E. L. Thorndike, B. F. Skinner, and Clark L. Hull. More specifically, we often refer to them as associationists. Thorndike brought forth ideas promoting a kind of connectionism: reliance on trial-and-error and development of good learning and social habits. To Thorndike the learning process included three important principles: (1) sensory "readiness" alluding to satisfaction obtained by completion of tasks; (2) mental exercise: strengthening through practice, repeated associations; and (3) effect: the concept that associations can be strengthened or weakened by consequences—concern for motivation, reward, or punishment.

Skinner compared respondent behavior (response brought about by some identifiable stimuli) with operant behavior (response without such identifiable stimuli). He believed that the desired response to a specific stimulus is indeed strengthened by immediate reinforcement, such as praise, recognition, and prizes.

Hull, like Skinner and Thorndike, promoted the concept of reinforcement. He believed that the best learning was that which resulted in, or came from reinforcement. Habit was to Hull an important component in his theory of "systematic behavior." Long before new technology and findings led to discovery of certain connections between brain chemicals and human behavior, Hull was considering the brain-success-pleasure factor. His thoughts of "joy in learning" and "the pleasure of success," among others certainly had validity.

As the behaviorists—or associationists—were concerned primarily with observable stimulus-response situations and dependent upon trial-and-error procedures as well as a practice of building up "good" habits that were based on learned responses, so the cognitivists were—and are—concerned with ideas, images, insights, problem solving, understanding of relationships, and drawing out relationships that are based on learned facts or related to credible assumptions.

Three important figures in the cognitive movement were Edward Tolman, Kurt Koffka, and Jean Piaget. Tolman's cognitive theory is goal oriented. Sign learning is the foundation in which the learner has options, or more than one way to reach the goal. Curriculum builders are familiar with sign learning, not only in terms of aims, goals, and objectives, but also with respect to logical organization and timelines for expected outcomes.

Kurt Koffka and other Gestalt psychologists emphasized the "characteristics of the whole," upon a relational pattern "which could not be explained as a sum of discrete and elementary sensory experiences (for instance, the melody which retains its identity despite transposition to another key). This was clearly at odds with the structuralists' contention that complex perceptions consist of a sensory core with a context of associated images and ideas" (Gibson, 28). In *Growth of the Mind* (1924), Koffka presented the Gestalt of cognition and the developmental process. Such processes, he stated, were of articulation and differentiation (Koffka, 1931: 380). In the Gestalt approach, as in other cognitive approaches, problem solving is achieved through reasoning and organization, with emphasis on intrinsic qualities. To bring forward some of these specific "characteristics of the whole" and also "relational patterns," I have highlighted below a recent study in which the authors have used melodies that retain their identities even when the key is transposed or various degrees of change are made by contour-preserving transformations, and transformation-preserving rhythm or rhythm and contour.

Study of Children's Perception of Musical Properties

The 1986 study, "Children's Perception of Certain Musical Properties: Scale and Contour," by Anne D. Pick and colleagues, University of Minnesota, was carried out as a five-part series. Employing simple melodies, the experimental tasks included judging transposed renditions of melodies, discriminating between transposed renditions of a melody, judging contour-preserving transformations of melodies, and also judging similarity to a familiar target melody of transformations preserving rhythm or rhythm and contour. "The ubiquity and complexity of music make the study of melody perception especially appealing since much of our knowledge of perception is based on relatively simple and static visual stimuli" (Pick et al., 1986: 3).

Studies One and Two demonstrated that young children detect key transposition in familiar melodies. The first two studies also provided evidence that children perceive the "sameness" of a melody that has been transposed in unfamiliar melodies as well as familiar ones. In Study Four the subjects learned to identify a target melody and distinguish it from a different set of melodies. They then heard the target melody with contour preserved and intervals changed. The researchers attempted to determine if the children heard the transformed version as being different from the target melody. Conditions included familiar and unfamiliar melodies. In Study Five, young children proved to be aware of "sameness" of the melody preserving contour even when used in a transformation. They could distinguish melodies that kept the same contour but had some change in the intervals.

Within the five studies, the researchers placed emphasis upon perception of similarities and differences, determination of familiar and unfamiliar melodies, similar or different structures—contour, intervals, rhythm patterns; these musical ideas and variations can be related by transformations that preserve the rhythm or the contour or the intervals of any theme in any possible combination. In the final part, Study Five, "Rudolph the Red-Nosed Reindeer" was the standard melody; two unfamiliar folk songs similar in length, but different in intervals, contour, and rhythm, and four transformations of "Rudolph" were used as the musical material. The first two transformations were composer-generated; they were similar to the standard melody in rhythm and contour, but had different intervals. The remaining two transformations were similar in rhythm, but differed in contour and intervals.

The children made similarity judgments by putting poker chips into three boxes—a red box for melodies "a lot like Rudolph," a pink box for melodies "a little like Rudolph," and a white box for melodies "not at all like Rudolph." The children participated individually, first listening to the "Rudolph" excerpt to assure that all subjects were very familiar with the song and were ready to proceed. The procedure was treated as a music game, with the purpose being to learn whether the songs sounded like "Rudolph."

The children listened to the six comparison melodies four times each. The melodies included the two rhythm-and-contour-preserving transformations of "Rudolph," the two rhythm-preserving transformations of "Rudolph," and the two folk songs differing from "Rudolph" in rhythm, contour, and intervals. The twenty-four melodies were presented in random order for all.

Transformations that preserved the rhythm and contour of "Rudolph" were judged more similar to it than were transformations that preserved only its rhythm. Thus, the children did perceive the invariant property of contour over transformations that preserved it. They can discern similarity between melodies that have the same contour, and they perceive that property across differences in intervals which distinguish between different melodies. (Pick, et al., 32–33)

The coauthors have much to say in their recap of the five studies. Their work herein remains fresh and valid in relation to the topic of this chapter, the arts and perception. Some of the most important findings from their closing general discussion are:

1. Young children can perceive similarities of transposed renditions of unfamiliar melodies.
2. They can distinguish between two renditions of a familiar melody in different keys.
3. They can distinguish between melodies with the same contour and rhythm but different intervals.
4. Children perceive the similarity of such melodies.
5. Children detect key transposition changes in familiar or unfamiliar melodies.
6. They are sensitive to melodic contour, and perceive relatedness of different melodies having the same contour.
7. Differentiation is a central process of perceptual learning.
8. Children display the ability to perceive some properties of the structure of melodies (Pick et al., 1986: 33–34).

In discussing perceptual style, we have focused on a radix which constantly confronts us with dualisms in form and effect. Most of the subject matter in this chapter in some way emphasizes dichotomies or pairs involving oppositional or compensatory concepts of phenomena or process such as light versus dark, voluntary versus involuntary, central versus diffuse, diluted versus saturated, field-dependent versus field-independent, or simple versus complex. Figure 2.1 brings together what aestheticians might consider as both the obvious yet ineffable. The combining of patterns of voluntary and involuntary actions in the human perceptual processes is no better illustrated than in the aesthetic experience.

I believe that it has become more essential than ever for educators in all fields to constantly remind themselves that teaching and learning involve both process and product. We have excellent opportunities for models of the many processes. As a result of the cognitive explosion and reliance on computer communication, we have become more aware of the difference between the products—data, solutions, accomplishments—and the processes—intellectual functioning and development.

Fig. 2.1
Schematic Representing Visual and Auditory Perception

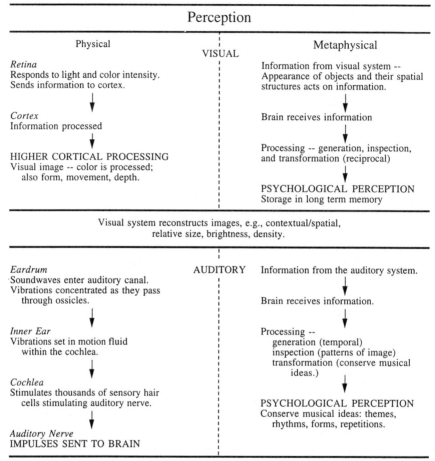

Perception		
Physical	VISUAL	Metaphysical
Retina Responds to light and color intensity. Sends information to cortex.		Information from visual system -- Appearance of objects and their spatial structures acts on information.
Cortex Information processed		Brain receives information
HIGHER CORTICAL PROCESSING Visual image -- color is processed; also form, movement, depth.		Processing -- generation, inspection, and transformation (reciprocal)
		PSYCHOLOGICAL PERCEPTION Storage in long term memory

Visual system reconstructs images, e.g., contextual/spatial,
relative size, brightness, density.

	AUDITORY	
Eardrum Soundwaves enter auditory canal. Vibrations concentrated as they pass through ossicles.		Information from the auditory system.
		Brain receives information.
Inner Ear Vibrations set in motion fluid within the cochlea.		Processing -- generation (temporal) inspection (patterns of image) transformation (conserve musical ideas.)
Cochlea Stimulates thousands of sensory hair cells stimulating auditory nerve.		PSYCHOLOGICAL PERCEPTION Conserve musical ideas: themes, rhythms, forms, repetitions.
Auditory Nerve IMPULSES SENT TO BRAIN		

Temporal system with stimulation to temporal cortex evokes clear memory of musical experience (object). Maximum phenomena representing authenticity of experience would be when subject actually hear (in the mind) the same piece of music, at the same place in the work, when given stimulation. Memory and linear experience become important parameters.

Critical thinking in the arts deeply involves the many facets of perception as presented in Figure 2.1. As we move on to the next chapter, it might be helpful to keep in mind this *schema* as we consider cognition and the numerous tandems of human processes which often involve the interface of perception and cognition. This area has become an enormous field of experience and study. In time, hopefully, all levels of educational programs will include the arts in all curricula that is dedicated to the development of cognitive skills.

3

Cognition and the Arts: Some Necessary Generalizations

We can hardly consider the subjects of critical thinking, creativity, and cognition as they apply to the arts, without reviewing some of the significant cognitive and behavioral theories from which many of us have drawn insights, conceptual reinforcements, and some much needed inspiration. As there exist valid theories and reports from hundreds of contemporary cognitivists and behaviorists, what appears in this section must be accepted as information from only a relatively small portion of experts past and present. Concepts and theories from the areas of psychology, neurosciences, education, and information theory have added greatly to the study of memory, learning, and cognition.

CONSERVATION

Eleanor Gibson, one of the outstanding scholars in the area of perception, has scrutinized and reported on Piaget's concept of "conservation." Gibson views the concept as intellectual achievement, and as such it is perfectly suited for application in the arts. She speaks of conservation as it applies to a quality of an object, its permanence or invariance. Recognition of patterns of variance or invariance in art objects is essential in the understanding of musical forms, poetry, dance, paintings, sculpture, and even architecture. Conservation may also apply to the properties of an object, for example, mass, speed, or volume. Conservation takes place more dramatically in the temporal arts, music and dance, than in the plastic arts. It occurs in symphony movements, for example, when the composer presents a main theme and then inserts a development section in which the main theme is varied or transformed but still retains enough of its basic qualities to be identified yet as the main theme extended or developed. Compositions entitled "theme and variations" also fit into this category: a main theme varied, extended, developed, with maybe as many as six, seven, or more variations. Many of the greatest compositions contain frequent examples of theme and variations. "In my opinion, conservation is invariance over time and over an event sequence; it is analogous to size and shape constancy over simple motions of the object and simple changes of the observer's point of view" (Gibson, 1969).

THE GESTALT, HUMAN PSYCHE, AND REAL ART

Koffka and Gestalt Theory

Beginning in 1930, when Gestalt theory was capturing the attention of American educators and psychologists, philosophers, artists, and aestheticians have been drawn to the topic. Its tenets appeared extremely adaptable to all areas of the arts, and, in fact, brought to life a new interest in related arts and aesthetic experience.

Gestalt concepts brought to the arts powerful models, metaphors, and analogies. In psychology, the Gestalt school, or approach, interprets phenomena as organized wholes rather than as groupings of distinct parts. It emphasizes that the significance of a structured whole does not depend entirely on its constituent parts. A painting, sculpture, or figure sketch, could have gaps or missing details and still have meaning. Gestalt concepts have become very important to aesthetics as well as to the study of personality, learning, memory, and thinking. Gestalt therapy relies on psychoanalysis and existential philosophy, focusing more on the present than the past. "By emphasizing newly emerging patterns (gestalten) that could become central to attention as part of a new whole of experience, it aims at changing the patient's habitual ways of perceiving and responding to needs. Much attention is given to nonverbal aspects of behavior" (Levey, 1983: 329). Of the three psychologists Kurt Koffka, Max Wertheimer, and Wolfgang Kohler, who led the Gestalt movement in the 1930s, Koffka probably became the most influential in the United States, because of his publications, *The Growth of the Mind* (1924) and *Principles of Gestalt Psychology* (1935).

To gain further connections of Gestalt theory and the aesthetic experience consider the following: (1) both deal with putting together parts to the whole; (2) both involve reasoning, organization, and internal or intrinsic qualities, which can become sources of pleasure; and (3) for both, a learning experience is organized through processes inherent in the learner and also through the immediate environment. A summation of the above three points might form a proposition for aesthetic identity as follows: In an aesthetic experience we must be sensitive to the parts; yet we must focus on how they fit into the total form (e.g., specific objects into a landscape or still life; specific sections into a final movement of a Mozart piano concerto), and enjoy confronting the work as an entity, being totally immersed in it, and at the same time, recalling associations that the mind brings forth to give the experience meaning as well as values to remember.

Abraham Moles contributed major studies (1958, 1966) that connected information theory to aesthetics, particularly to the aesthetics of music because of its auditory and temporal character. Moles and his contemporaries presented researchers with models that relate to various aspects of information theory, such as the Markov processes, reticular (network-like) patterns—models that might accommodate both theoretical and empirical data in explaining such phenomena in music listening as novelty, familiarity, satiation, conditioning, and guessing.

SCHEMA

Jean Piaget's concept of the spiral developmental sequence from infancy through adolescence had by 1960 become ensconced in both the educational and child development communities. His four major stages of development of thought processes are as follows: (1) sensorimotor (first 18 months); (2) preoperational (1–7 years); (3) concrete operations (7–12 years); and (4) formal operations (12 years through adulthood). Piaget approached perception as a constructive process, yet treated it differently from cognition. Perception depends on sensory information and actually involves assimilation of such sensory input.

Piaget and Children's Musical Development

Below is a brief outline of Jean Piaget's psychology of intelligence as it pertains to developmental learning and, specifically, to the spiral curriculum. In chapter five, further discussion of the subject focuses on the work of Marilyn Pflederer Zimmerman and Piaget's theory of conservation as it applies to music.

Sensori-Motor (birth–2 years)

Pre-Operational (1.5–7 years)
    rudimentary use of symbols
    egocentric orientation to symbols

Concrete (7–12 years)
    thinking no longer dependent solely on perceptions
    able to draw more relationships

Formal (13 years and beyond)
    now both qualitative and quantitative applications
    envisioning hypothetical situations/relations
    verifying relations
    conservation and reversibility

Jerome Bruner, like Piaget, emphasized perception as having some qualities closely akin to cognition. Work of Bartlett (1932) and Vernon (1954, 1955) has influenced thought of Piaget and Bruner in the concept of the schema. Schema = model, classification of past experiences, which have mediated the perception of objects in the environment. As receptors of the cortex receive different qualities and variations in sensory patterns as well as various combinations of sensory patterns and subsequent integration of them, these result in new constructions or forms. These new constructions systematically become part of new concepts, which we label as schemata (Vernon, 1954: 14). During perceptual processing, schemata tell the observer what sensory data to select, what to expect, and also how to classify and name the data.

What Piaget and Bruner designated as perceptual learning and perceptual development when applied to aesthetic experiences seems to become a gray area, difficult to differentiate between cognition and perception, not by definition, but rather by application to such specifics as memory and attention. In Gibson's watershed text on the subject, *Principles of Perceptual Learning and Development* (1969), aestheticians have found a premier resource of the theories, trends, and general disposition of information about perception and cognition for the past century as it might relate to phenomena and experiences in the arts. Gibson has thoroughly covered the concept of the schema since Bartlett (1932).

Gibson (1969: 46–52) builds on the fact that Piaget distinguishes sharply between perception and rational or intellectual processes that follow "rules of logic." To Piaget, cognitive development involves various combinations of perception with the intellectual processes. The perception then involves assimilation of sensory input directed to a schema, and, with this action, this schema becomes dedicated to a specific art object. Gibson agrees with Piaget that this building a schema in the mind is a fundamental process, a very necessary process of perceptual learning. I believe that this reinforces my conjecture that the aesthetic transaction relies on a combination of cognitive and perceptual processes.

Bruner, Piaget's foremost proponent in the United States in the area of education and child development, like Piaget, believes that all perception relies upon categorization. Gibson (1969: 49) cites the importance of several stages of this categorization: (1) primitive, a perceptual isolation of an art object or event, or parts thereof; (2) search for cues; and (3) a type of closure in which the object or event and its characteristics or qualities are confirmed, and the cue searching is terminated instinctively rather than cognitively. The more categories we have to rely on, the more perceptual readiness we have. According to Bruner (1951), "The hypotheses which the observer applies in his search for cues might, presumably, reflect his personal needs, values, and personality patterns." This is an extremely important and relevant point in regard to the arts in terms of preference, motivation, even pleasure and habit.

States of need might dictate the broadness—even pleasure responses—and accessibility of a person's categories, what Gibson refers to as "a notion which had much to do with the so-called new look research in perception" (Gibson, 1969: 50).

METACOGNITION

R. J. Sternberg's ideas represent one of the more recent of trends in the study of learning processes: metacognition, or higher-order thinking. Sternberg has attempted to outline valid paradigms of higher order processes. Such higher order thinking has direct application to the arts, particularly the temporal aspects of music and dance. In *Higher Order Reasoning in Postformal Operational Thought*, Sternberg reports on research findings which suggest the importance of the ability to perceive and understand abstract relations to intelligence. The findings also infer that this ability increases with age, from adolescence on. This ability is determined to be part of a cognitive/metacognitive thinking, forming higher-order concepts and principles (relations).

Most researchers in this area, like Sternberg, have been greatly influenced by Piaget in the developmental approach of their theories. Sternberg posits that the age groups of five to fourteen probably develop concepts through rote learning mainly of stimulus-response relations; and the older subjects use higher order thinking as a basis for reasoning. To Sternberg, intellectual development centers on what is called "second-degree operations," that is, understanding relations between relations, analogical reasoning ability, as expressed in the following theory.

Theory of Higher Order Reasoning by Analogy

Higher order reasoning begins with what can be designated as analogies of the second-order, such as, A:B :: C:D, or Bench: Judge :: Pulpit: Minister (A is to B as C is to D, or Bench is to Judge as Pulpit is to Minister). Sternberg asserts that such second-order analogies can be understood in terms of basic components of information processing such as:

1. *Encoding*—retrieving relevant semantic attributes from long-term memory

2. *Inference*—ordering the analogy components

3. *Mapping*—discovering second-order associations for connecting

4. *Application*—focus on correlates (corresponding elements)

5. *Justification*—checking validity of order

6. *Response*—evaluation of "goodness" of analogy

7. *Association*

We deal with higher-order thinking every day whenever we take time to reflect on some idea, concept, or problem. There are those who think that a painter paints and a composer writes music by some kind of instinct and intuition along with emotion. While those processes and qualities are there, much more is necessary; not only cognition, but metacognition or higher-order thinking and reasoning goes into it, and the great pleasure that goes with it can be overwhelming at times. Thus, with the arts we can always count on involving our minds and senses, invoking associations, sometimes listening, performing, painting, viewing, sculpting, drawing, and dancing, or simply talking about the arts, or thinking about thinking.

FUSION OF PERCEPTION AND COGNITION

In chapter two, within the discussion of perceptual style and specifically, field dependence/independence, I emphasized the concern that in arts or aesthetic processes, perceptual style applies to certain intellectual (cognitive) activities, as well as the perceptual. In that chapter I mentioned the ongoing study, *Cognitive Events Referenced to Stimuli Produced by Specific Music Listening Experiences: Creative/Critical Thinking and Eidetic Imagery.* The review of the study in chapter four will emphasize the need for identification and understanding of both speculative and verifiable components in the aesthetic transaction. Five important terms in any consideration of aesthetic process are defined below. These terms become increasingly meaningful to us in our connections between perception and cognition.

1. *Cognition*—those mental processes that include attention via perception, memory, analysis, synthesis—those activities involved in learning and creativity. Thinking.

2. *Eidetic imagery*—pertaining to visual imagery retained in the memory and readily reproducible with various degrees of accuracy, and sometimes with great detail. This study does not acknowledge any evidence of eidetic imagery as relative to any phenomenon that might be designated as "photographic memory."

3. *Program music*—instrumental music that often has some contextual references (usually very general) relating to some literary or pictorial source. Programmatic compositions, therefore, rely upon "extra-musical ideas," which the composers, themselves, have indicated. They involve many different degrees of imagery on the part of the listener.

4. *Field dependence*—perceptual style in which the subject's perception is strongly dominated by the overall organization of the surrounding field, and parts of the field are experienced as "fused" (Witkin et al., 1971).

5. *Field independence*—perceptual style in which parts of the field are experienced as discrete from organized ground (Witkin).

Musical processes present us with ample background for this concept of fusion of perception and cognition. Complex musical events can be divided into three classifications: creating, performing, and receiving (listening). All involve certain degrees of critical thinking. Over the past several decades the increased emphasis on cognitive processes in music listening as well as performance and composing has led some psychologists as well as music researchers to attach much more significance to the musical experience as an important part of human perception and learning.

The study of eidetic imagery as aesthetic function and phenomenon—thus critical thinking—finds its way to the arts through both psychology and philosophy. Current research and related literature emphasize eidetic imagery as not generally related to memory ability itself, not "photographic memory," but an isolated curiosity. If we approach eidetic imagery as both a critical thinking process and a creative process, we can with some assurance relate it to more specific examples of cognitive effects such as those of certain listening experiences. As we consider the image and the process of imaging in chapter four, we will draw upon the research of a broad spectrum of scholars such as Michael Tye (1991), who insist on the generalization that imaging must exist at two levels, empirical and metaphysical. Such a generalization has remained the center of very fruitful debate, research, and interdisciplinary study, as well as serious scientific and philosophic developments in the areas of aesthetics.

CREATIVITY AND THE COGNITIVE-AFFECTIVE PROCESS

While the term "creativity in the arts" might seem to be a redundancy to many artists, musicians, dancers, poets, aestheticians, and philosophers, modern psychology literature frequently refers to various creative modes and processes in which specific cognitive processes are joined by, and influenced by, specific affective processes which join together within various creative efforts (Russ, 1993).

We in the arts generally accept one as hand-in-hand with the other. We think universally of creativity as something connected with only the best of individuals, and the current research literature distinguishes between the creative product and the creative process. Creative products are generally unique or original, or novel, and must be aesthetically pleasing and useful as an object of value or representation of value.

One might ask if value, uniqueness, and novelty, are to be judged according to standards of a particular discipline. Can value be judged beyond the discipline? And, must there be a "newness" in the product? Most scholars involved in study and research on creativity would agree that the answers would be yes. According to Russ, "A product is creative if old facts are integrated in new ways, new relationships emerge from old ideas, or there is a new configuration" (1993: 2).

Although "newness" or novelty would not be the only thing to look for in a creative product, it can safely be considered as an important element.

However, the novelty factor can involve restructuring as much as something "brand new"—variations, changes, old items in "new dress." In attempting to develop valid comprehensive definition of creativity, Russ seeks a consensus of opinion, one in which there appears reference to capacity to produce original ideas, insights, restructuring, "inventions or artistic objects which are accepted by experts as being of a scientific, aesthetic, social, or technological value" (Russ, 2). She reiterates the commonplace dilemma of judging whether or not something is of true creative value and states that cultural values and norms are an "inevitable part of the criteria for judging something to be creative." If a creative work is good, but much ahead of its time—this could involve any number of issues, for example, subject matter, style, and technical aspects—and is not recognized as a valid or acceptable work, the two aforementioned criteria, cultural values and norms, would seem to conflict. "Something might be so new that it breaks the rules of the discipline by which something is judged to be good, and time is needed for the standards to catch up with the advance in the field" (Russ, 2, 58–63). The previous statement is probably valid when applied to the areas of science, business, and industry. However, the arts do not fit easily into any such pattern. Chapters five and seven will include a substantial amount of material presenting several aspects of values theory.

We do not have to approach the question of artistic/aesthetic quality of an art work at the same time we are recognizing its level of creativity. Although the great masterpieces of the centuries in painting, sculpture, architecture, music, poetry, and literature at certain moments in history might have been extolled for their newness, novelty, or originality, they were not necessarily judged specifically on those qualities. In any survey of any of the art fields, one can find the qualities and the mechanics that would seem to favor sameness and invariants. Examples of such work might be found in those periods that were most enduring and artistically fecund: pre-Christian Greek—Doric, Ionic, and Corinthian architecture; late Medieval—Romanesque-Gothic cathedral architecture, iconic religious paintings and statuary; fourteenth, fifteenth, and sixteenth centuries—motets, mass settings of France, Italy, and madrigals of England and Italy; eighteenth century—European dance forms; eighth to nineteenth centuries—Japanese traditional Gagaku (ritualistic, instrumental, and vocal) and Hogaku (vocal music mainly, stereotyped melody patterns when used in connection with Kabuki).

Stages of Creativity

Researchers such as Wallas (1926), Armbruster (1989), and Russ (1993) have considered the concept of a four-stage model of the creative process: (1) information gathering; (2) idea development and free association; (3) illumination and solution; and (4) solution evaluated (critical thinking and logic dominant here). Within these four stages, the significance of logic, memory, and abstract thinking becomes apparent.

J. P. Guilford, one of the first investigators to connect creativity with cognitive processes, has contributed to a better understanding of critical thinking, creativity, and talent as they relate to art experiences. After twenty years of research and reporting in the areas of personality, intelligence, and creativity, he published two works, *The Nature of Human Intelligence* (1967) and *Intelligence, creativity, and their educational implications* (1968) in which he emphasizes that creative processes are experienced by almost all individuals in a normal population. Other points of interest and relevance to the arts are his arguments and data implying that the arts and the sciences have process similarities, most notably in the area of tasks in problem solving.

Divergence and Convergence

Guilford's inferential data and hypotheses that intelligence tests measure processes reflecting convergent thinking, and that creative thinking generally reflects divergent thinking processes, seems acceptable. However, this might become something of an exaggeration when applied to creativity in the arts. For instance, composers of larger music forms will need to constantly rely on the convergent as well as the divergent. Even when composers are seeking new sounds, they start with traditional patterns and processes with which they are already well acquainted. Likewise, painters who might be included among the most avant-garde, the most revolutionary, will rely on some of the most traditional and "acceptable" modes and styles of forms, hue blends, manner, and use of complimentary hues. Sculptors who produce abstract works use "consensus" modes and means even when working with experimental mediums.

CREATIVITY AND SIGNIFICANT FIGURES IN THE ARTS

As we focus on the above statements, let us turn our attention to specific examples, several significant figures in the arts, Americans and others whose work greatly influenced the direction of twentieth-century American arts and culture.

Composers

Aaron Copland, as the United States "All American" composer (born in Brooklyn, N. Y., 1900) became a model for other serious American composers seeking new musical expressions that would be freer of European traditions. Yet, his style and creative effort were generally traditional, of a consensus nature; he employed musical forms that stood the test of time with the exception of two aspects: harmony and national social context. Copland introduced quartal harmony, often building chords with intervals of the fourth—and fourths upon fourths—rather than the traditional thirds, fifths, octaves, and sevenths. The more global aspect, national context, was as important as the quartal harmony for innovation and divergence. In the following list of selected compositions by Copland, note the titles and their Americana references:

Dance Symphony (1929)	Some jazz references
Piano Variations (1930)	Ragtime references
El Salon Mexico (1936)	Ballet*
Billy the Kid (1938)	Ballet*
Rodeo (1942)	Ballet*
Appalachian Spring (1943)	Ballet*
A Lincoln Portrait (1942)	Narrator and orchestra
Symphony No. 3 (1944)	Quartal harmony emphasized
Clarinet Concerto (1948)	Jazz idioms
The Tender Land (1954)	Copland's only opera

*All four ballets have heavy emphasis on quartal harmony.

After a few years of study in New York City, Copland spent the years 1921–24 in Paris for study with Nadia Boulanger. During those Paris years, he came under the influence of Stravinsky's work. Even then with his cosmopolitan education and Parisian insight into the arts, Copland was determined to write music which would be totally American. He incorporated popular styles, jazz, and patriotic or historical Americana into almost all of his works. His development of a kind of "everyday music," works for high school performance and study, "Music for Radio," and five musical scores for movies, kept him in touch with the American public in almost all quarters. His musical score for the film *The Heiress* (1948) won an Academy Award.

As Aaron Copland was a model for young American composers by 1940, so Igor Stravinsky (1882–1971) was a model of worldwide proportions by 1930. Stravinsky, the musical icon figure for the new sweeping modernism of the early twentieth century, presents to us this ubiquitous dilemma we encounter again and again: works that are incited and incubated through creative processes that are equally divergent and convergent. Perhaps this is the reason that we find in any of the larger arts survey texts such frequent usage of the prefix "neo", as in neoclassic, neoromantic, neomodern. This becomes an important point of semantics, as early on in the century, Stravinsky was described as a neoclassicist. Not only did he prefer and master classic forms; he voiced appreciation for the music of Haydn, Beethoven, and Tchaikovsky, as well as other masters of the Baroque, Classic, and Romantic eras. I sincerely believe that this is a most pleasing dilemma of cognition, creativity, and critical thinking found much more in the arts over the centuries than in science, business, or manufacturing. By 1910, Stravinsky had already gained fame in Europe with the success of his first ballet, *The Firebird*. In 1913 he added to his fame, but also drew controversy with his ballet, *The Rite of Spring*, a work with such primitive drive, dissonance, and revolutionary scoring, that it caused a near-riot at the Paris Opera House during its first performance. In 1939, Stravinsky came to the United States from Russia, and in 1945 he became an American citizen.

I use here the work of Stravinsky to further elaborate upon the relative importance of divergence and convergence to be found in creative actions. Well before Stravinsky's death in 1971, scholars were analyzing and appraising the modern master's work. Stravinsky's use of conventional patterns was often a main topic, as the use of convention by a composer perceived by many as being extremely unconventional was certainly a hot issue. Edward Cone began such an analysis with a statement that great composers, no matter of what era, often chose conventional patterns of an earlier time in which to work and define their musical ideas, no matter how novel they might be. He cited the Viennese Classics of the eighteenth and nineteenth centuries as examples: "A composer may deliberately defeat the expectations aroused by the specific pattern followed; the resulting tension between anticipated and actual course of the music can be a source of esthetic delight. This is the way Stravinsky has used conventions of the past, but it is important to realize that the composers of the periods of interest to him have also played with their own conventions" (Cone, 1963: 21). The author goes on to explain how Stravinsky employs a classical model of the symphony (Stravinsky's Symphony in C), such as would have been used by Haydn, Mozart, or Beethoven. He states that the composer, even like some of his eighteenth-century counterparts, would choose to make subtle or even glaring alterations along the way, hoping that "the more alert among his listeners might gain added enjoyment from the interplay of the anticipated and the actual" (Cone, 24).

Certainly the traditional framework is emphasized here: the Classical orchestral layout, the diatonic melodies, the metric regularity, the apparent harmonic simplicity, the ostensibly typical patterns. At the same time, any expectation of a work easily comprehensible in a comfortably familiar idiom is defeated, even for the most sanguine hearer, by certain immediately perceptible features: the distinctive instrumental sound; the persistent, though mild, dissonance; the sudden harmonic shifts . . . Now, the simple filling-out of a Classical mold with contemporary stuffing could produce nothing more important than a parody in the manner of Prokofiev, but Stravinsky's intent is serious. He confronts the evoked historical manner at every point with his own version of contemporary language; the result a complete reinterpretation and transformation of the earlier style. (Cone, 25)

Stravinsky was an eclectic; yet, even with his use of many past forms, styles, and ideas, he transformed them to fit his own needs. His *Rite of Spring* reflected the postromantic character in which the composer referred often to his Russian heritage through the use of folk melodies or folk-like melodies. Although shockingly dissonant and full of strange rhythmic ideas unfamiliar to the audience of 1913, the work did not reach the atonal complexities of serialism and renewal of classic form, or the use of jazz idioms as his later works would. (For teaching examples, see chapter six.)

Before we leave this discussion, which has brought together several musical concepts related to creativity, newness and novelty, tradition and convention, it seems logical to reinforce the perspectives of some cultural similarities, as the first four decades of the twentieth century gave us the era of Ragtime and Gershwin. We have already discussed the significance of Copland and Stravinsky in the mainstream of modern American music, and we know of their interest in and influence from jazz idioms; but this discussion would not be complete without devoting some attention to an individual who had a defining influence on American music: George Gershwin (b. Brooklyn, N.Y., 1898). Even with his unfortunately short life span (d. Hollywood, 1937), he left his mark on both Europe and America. In the United States, even more than in Europe and South America, there was by 1920 a search for a national identity in music. With the new music more and more released from European dominance, Gershwin became the figurehead of the trend to bring together popular and concert elements. At the age of eighteen he was already one of America's most successful popular song writers, an icon of Tin Pan Alley and Broadway as well as the jazz scene. However, Gershwin, the songwriter and jazz pianist, was also a serious composer. He was indeed the first composer to bring jazz, Tin Pan Alley, and Broadway into the concert halls of America and Europe. Such works as the Concerto in F, *An American in Paris*, and *Rhapsody in Blue* established for Gershwin an important place among the twentieth-century composers.

Painters

Obviously, we can go far back into history to find multitudes of artists who were revolutionary, "ahead of their times," yet used "traditional" subjects, media, and forms, for example, Botticelli, El Greco, and Rembrandt, to name a few. Even limiting our focus to more recent periods, we can find numerous such examples, including Picasso, O'Keeffe, Monet, and the American Impressionists.

At the beginning of the twentieth century the group of painters who would more nearly represent divergence in their creative efforts than any others of their time were the Fauves (including Matisse, Rouault, Derain, and Braque) whose work took the form of a kind of expressionism in which were found distortion of traditional forms and excessive exuberance of color. This small-scale trend existed for only a few years around the turn of the century, yet is considered to represent the true beginning of twentieth-century modern painting. Fauvism influenced other painters, particularly Wassily Kandinsky, a Russian, who went beyond Fauvism into very new and radical departures. Around 1910, at the same time that German composers were making equally radical departures from the musical establishment, Kandinsky totally abandoned representation in his paintings. Immersed in abstract forms, he often attempted to eliminate any or all resemblance to the physical world. This abstraction process (pulling out from, separating) became the foundation of much of the new modern art. Was Kandinsky at this point, by definition and description, more creative than Picasso, at least within the concept of divergence? (We will come back to this point at the end of this chapter.)

Pablo Picasso (1881–1973), leaving his native Spain for Paris in 1900, completed during the first decade of the new century the works of his Blue and Rose periods. We know that Picasso was anti-expressionist early on, but later in life he became more experimental and, on occasion, more expressionistic. Most significant was his sensitivity to, and mastery of, formalism. Even though he could convey violence and cynicism, derision and bitterness in his works, that emotion or expressionism seldom overshadowed his closeness to form and structure. This formalism furnished the drive for Picasso's output, as with Stravinsky's musical forms. Picasso methodically sought out references to form and organization of past masters. During his neoclassic period, in works such as *Mother and Child, Harlequin, Standing Nude*, and *Three Musicians*, this formalism is dominant, but it is now Picasso's. It belongs to him. From 1915 to 1930 his figures are strong; arms are often elongated, hands, legs, and feet very large, bodies are generally solid. "By 1920, he was working simultaneously in two separate styles: collage Cubism and a Neoclassic style of strongly modeled, heavy-bodied figures such as his Mother and Child . . . he needed to resume contact with the classical tradition, the 'art of the museums' " (Janson and Kerman, 1977).

Although Picasso's work greatly influenced American painters, it had far less impact than did Monet and the French Impressionists. Only a small number of eighteenth-century American artists had produced nature scenes; their interest was in human figures, portraits, commemorative scenes, and still life studies. However, an amazing abundance of talented landscapists sprang upon the scene toward the end of the nineteenth century with large numbers of canvases which revealed not only an intense appeal for nature, but also creative insights resulting from carefully observed effects of nature in color, light, and atmosphere. First came the early and mid-nineteenth-century classical naturalist (realist) painters, including Frederic Church, Thomas Cole, George Inness, Winslow Homer, and Thomas Eakins; then, at the turn of the century, there came to prominence large numbers of artists who were almost to a person to become part of the movement of American Impressionism, notably Theodore Robinson, Childe Hassam, Joseph DeCamp, Frank Benson, John

Twachtman, William Merritt Chase, Willard Metcalf, J. Alden Weir, Edmund Tarbell, Thomas Dewing, Edward Simmons, and Ernest Lawson. Other painters who might not have professed adherence to the impressionist principles in toto, but shared many of the same perspectives, included John Singer Sargent, Mary Cassatt, George Noyes, N. C. Wyeth, William Chadwick, and William Glackens.

During the nineteenth century, thousands of American artists studied in Paris. At the turn of the century, and for two more decades, many more artists also made the pilgrimage to Giverny, the home and studio of Claude Monet. By 1905 the leaders of American Impressionism, Childe Hassam and Theodore Robinson, had been "converted" to Impressionism while in France. It is true that both artists developed styles in which creative production was certainly their own. However, all of their aesthetic foundation was fashioned by their French experiences. Their creative efforts were often simple transformations of the new French effects: momentary effects produced by sunlight (usually overstatements), and juxtaposed pure colors.

Tonalism was a movement that flourished in America from about 1880 to about 1915, devoted primarily to landscape painting and related to late Barbizon manifestations in France and the United States. The artists who practiced it were most concerned with poetic evocations of nostalgia and reverie, accomplished either by the domination of one color—especially gray, gold, or blue—over all others or by the emphasis on a colored atmosphere or mist through which forms were perceived, often dimly, and which produced an evenness of hue throughout. (Gerdts, 1984: 14)

Our thesis is constant: the creativity of the early American Impressionists was early on very convergent, then transformational, and finally divergent in such styles as tonalism, glare effect (exaggerated play of light), and outlining (drawn outlines) that went beyond outlining of shapes with light, shadow, or color, as in the brilliant watercolors of Maurice Prendergast. (For an excellent comprehensive display of Prendergast watercolors and oils, see Gerdts, *American Impressionism*, 1984.)

The period from 1900 through 1920 had been a highly productive time for American Impressionist painters. Even though many artists were taking up new ideas and considering new directions, the Impressionist movement remained strong for the simple reason that the American aesthetic of the time included a sense of well managed eclecticism, a spirit that allowed a strong Impressionist movement to continue, coexisting with two new directions: formalist modernism (including fauvism and cubism), and urban realism. A strong case-in-point of this broad technical and emotional development is the creativity of Ernest Lawson (1873–1939). Lawson, like Prendergast, though generally part of the Impressionist movement, never allied himself as deeply with its aesthetic aims as did "The Ten." For twenty years The Ten held exhibitions exclusively of the group members, mostly in New York and Boston.

Lawson, an urban realist, combined many of the newer aesthetic concepts of The Ten; yet he was not, and is not considered an eclectic. His creative style included impressionistic approaches to form, light, and color, yet also expressed symbolism and other aspects that appeared to be his own. His 1916 oil on canvas, *Segovia*, evinces what critics referred to as a lyrical quality. More important, according to Gerdts, it "took on a more dramatic chiaroscuro and yet became more geometric than his other works, hinting at Cezannesque structure." Later in his life, in the early 1930s, Lawson even produced some expressionistic works during annual visits to Florida (Gerdts, 275–279).

We have been concerned with two approaches, divergent and convergent, in defining creativity, or at least in considering levels of creativity. I have saved the discussion of Georgia O'Keeffe until last among the painters, as I believe that she, of all the artists mentioned in this chapter, retained the most divergent creative qualities throughout her life. O'Keeffe's paintings do not seek truth, but simply a way of seeing, a deep appreciation for nature.

A major influence on O'Keeffe during her student days was the work of the Russian abstractionist Wassily Kandinsky, particularly the concepts that center on relationships between music and visual art derived from his book *Concerning the Spiritual in Art*. Kandinsky attached a spiritual vibration to each color, and maintained that "artists must first discover their most innermost feelings and necessities and then create forms and colors that capture these essences" (Castro, 1985: 12). At age forty-seven, O'Keeffe came under the spell of the New Mexico landscape, specifically the severe geophysical land forms. In a study by Jane Collins cited in Castro, she presents what she believes to be O'Keeffe's twenty-one stylistic traits ingrained in her New Mexico landscapes, both abstract and realist. Seven of them, I believe, are germane to our considerations:

1. an interest in ordinary and unspectacular features of the landscape.
2. compositions consisting of horizontal bands of contrasting colors.
3. a preference for flat, even lighting so that forms are fully illuminated and not obscured by shadows.
4. the suppression of individual brushstrokes to achieve a restrained and nongestural surface except for some interplay of rough and smooth textures.
5. the total exclusion from the landscape of people, animals or anything made by man.
6. a static, motionless, timeless quality.
7. an attraction to sculptured, rounded, sensual shapes.

The general public thinks of O'Keeffe's repertory as mainly consisting of flowers and sand dunes, but this is not the case; some of her finest creative efforts emphasize form or structure and abstract shapes. One of O'Keeffe's most impressive works of this type is *East River from the 30th Story of the Shelton Hotel, New York* (1928). It consists of combinations of formal patterns that comprise many shapes and many hues and values—something like abstraction and representation together, the abstractness come to life.

O'Keeffe's art contains richly colored forms—abstract shapes, flowers, buildings, bones, hills, trees, clouds, sky, and stones—variously characterized in large, clean patterns that are now her trademark. The brilliant, but sometimes uneven, quality of her work and her innovations in technique, theme, and style are central to her remarkable career as an artist. (Castro, 59–75)

Many art critics and scholars have written about the strong underlying sexual metaphors in O'Keeffe's paintings and sculpture with reserve and respect, rather than show any great negative concern, understanding that those metaphors were truly part of the style, the form and structure of her work, often divergent, but relevant, creativity.

Sculptors

The British sculptor Henry Moore (1898–1986), is familiar to the American public; many of his sculptures are in permanent museum and gallery collections in the United States. Like other twentieth-century sculptors, he employed cubism to various degrees. His bronze cast *Family Group* (1950) "typifies a style of organic free forms with just enough objectivity to be representational" (Wold, 1987: 287–88). Although some might look upon this sculpture as primitive, it is important to recognize and understand are some of the characteristics identifying Moore's style: smooth, rounded forms that symbolize the basic shapes of the human figure. In *Family Group*, we can find formal unity among the figures, a unity that not only strengthens the form, but also gives an emotional and expressive idea of the family unit (Wold, 287).

Moore believed that the viewer of a piece of sculpture, to be truly sensitive to the aesthetic significance of the artwork must "learn to feel shape simply as shape, not as description or reminiscence." He must, for example, perceive an egg as a simple single solid shape, quite apart from its significance as food, or from the literary idea that it will become a bird" (Dudley, 1978). Moore was not, however, discounting associations or the possibility of some contextual meaning. In his own words, Moore suggested that the viewer not consider his sculpture's shapes and forms as ends in themselves: "I am very much aware that associational, psychological factors play a large part in sculpture. The meaning and significance of form itself probably depend on the countless associations of man's history." He went on to say that certain shapes and forms convey certain ideas to viewers according to their habits of perception (Dudley, 1978: 33). Research studies tell us that habits of perception can be observed in very young children, and can be reinforced and extended as the children grow and mature. "I think the humanist organic element [i.e., abstraction] will always be for me of fundamental importance in sculpture, giving sculpture its vitality" (Dudley, 40).

Constantin Brancusi (1876–1957) produced sculptures that were considered to relate to the older, more traditional style; yet his work has been described by many as tending "toward the outer limits of abstraction" (Vyverberg, 311). Americans know Brancusi mainly through his sculpture, *Bird in Space*, of which he made over two dozen versions, each with minor differences or modifications; for example, some were polished bronze, others stainless steel, some larger than others. Millions of Americans over the past seventy years have viewed the versions of *Bird in Space* in the Philadelphia Museum of Art (1925) and also the Museum of Modern Art in New York (1928). It is an abstraction of the representation of a bird's feather as it evokes the idea of a soaring bird. (See photo of *Bird in Space* in chapter five.)

The creative approach of both sculptors could be labeled as both divergent and convergent. Their creativity relied on models and concepts already in existence; yet they extended their creative efforts beyond known forms.

4

The Image Is Everything

In recent years a new emphasis on experimental imagery has arisen within the area of cognitive studies. As part of cognitive science, imagery as a process of the brain and "mind" has surfaced after more than fifty years of disregard or neglect. Areas of research include studies which depend on data captured by electrophysiological means: electromyography, electroencephalograms, magnetic scanners, etc., as well as studies of only a descriptive nature. Very little activity in this specific kind of empirical research has been initiated by arts scholars and practitioners. Psychologists with interest in music, such as Carl Seashore, have led the way since the early 1930s. Hazel Stanton's "Eastman Experiment," Measurement of Musical Talent (1935) includes consideration of the concept of tonal memory. Since that time a very thin, but nevertheless continuous, progression of study has involved researchers in music and visual arts as well as psychology and neuroscience, taking up such topics as: tonal memory, eidetic imagery, affective response and images, measurement of aesthetic awareness, etc.

IMAGERY AND THE GREAT DEBATE

Four Questions

Do images exist? Some cognitive scientists maintain that the question of whether or not mental images exist is "a conflation of several issues, none of which involves imagery in any important way . . . One can take 'mental image' to denote experiences, or internal (neural) representations, or even intentional objects" (Block, 1981: 5–6). More specific answers to this question will be generated from and depend on answers from the remaining three questions.

Are mental images only symptomatic? This is an interesting question within the arts. Unlike in medicine, technology, social sciences, or certain areas of philosophy, it makes little or no difference in visual or temporal arts whether or not the images are secondary, even when accounting for quality or value. We can accept as obvious the need in medical sciences and technologies for true perception, not because practitioners seek the truth, but because they seek real things, real conditions, status, data, etc. No place exists in medicine for planning and management of surgical assignments on fantasy, no matter how nice the release from reality might make everyone involved feel at a given moment. The stark realities of the medical case, no matter whether they be pleasant, dramatic or dismal, must be clear. Not so with the arts. Only two realities need to exist: (1) the reality of the medium (color, sound, wood, plaster, movement, and so on); and (2) what I choose to denote as the "reality of determined origination," the recognition of the art object being generated by the artist's mind or copied or fashioned by that artist from the product of someone else's mind.

Are representations in imagery equal to those in perception? Although this question, like the previous one, has little application to the arts in terms of quality or value, it is extremely important in another way. The more important issue here is that through our powers of perception we see, hear, touch, and smell; but through our powers of imagery we bring into play representations that rely on memory of seeing, hearing, touching, and smelling, or any such combination of those senses made necessary at a given moment by a specific aesthetic experience.

Can mental images be scanned? This takes on some importance in all of the arts in terms of creativity/critical thinking, and determination of the level of vividness of the imagery, which brings us to the points of difference between pictorial and descriptional representation. When we speak of any descriptionist approach to experiences in the arts, we find very little resistance to its ideas and concepts among scientists, philosophers, and the general public, as the descriptionalist view is that our mental images represent in the manner of language rather than pictures. The pictorialist view, however, meets with much more resistance because although "the pictorialists agree that we don't literally have pictures in our brains," they steadfastly insist, nevertheless, "that our mental images represent in roughly the way that pictures represent" (Block 1981: 2–8). Thus, in limiting our discussion to the arts, we can say that images can be scanned, and that both sides of the argument can be right at times, leaving the issue in a strange sense of concurrence.

In psychology, neuroscience, as well as philosophy of science, there seem to remain some serious questions. Block believes that the stakes are high in the imagery debate for psychology: "The question whether the representations of imagery are pictorial or descriptional is not straightforwardly empirical but is one of those problems where everything is up for grabs, including precisely what the problem is" (Block, 1981: 3–4). He admits that to the general public this is probably a very obscure issue, one that might lead us to ask if and why it is worthy of our attention. Then he proceeds to emphasize that this "bone of contention" of the relative importance of, and distinction between, the pictorial and descriptional views is important in many areas of cognitive psychology. Numerous studies are giving experimental support through mental image prototypes. The nature of mental images is closely connected to the question of the nature of human thought.

If the pictorialist view is correct, the human brain is capable of processing any number of representations of a kind not found in digital computers, those digital examples considered as paradigms of descriptional representation. The computer can only simulate; it cannot actually process information in the manner of humans (Block, 4). This is a critical point: there is no spectrum of life in which this is more important than within the arts. The human capacity to bring into being pristine ideas, forms, and expressions, shards of light and color, and darkness; the capacity, itself, for retaining, relating, generating, far outshadows any effects of human-made machines.

Pictorialists and Descriptionalists

"There has been a remarkable revival of interest in mental imagery among psychologists after a long period of neglect. It is now considered respectable again to talk of people having mental images and to inquire into their role in cognition" (Tye, 1991: xi). Within the confines of this academic debate, those leading proponents of the pictorial view, such as Stephen Kosslyn, believe that their approach allows for more proof through experimentation than does that of the descriptionalists. Unlike most cognitive scientists, those of us connected with the arts—in practice, philosophy, or theory—probably embrace both approaches, as hopefully, the statements on these next few pages will help to substantiate.

Theories of Michael Tye and S. M. Kosslyn (see Tye, 1991: 34–43) might help us to point toward more specific application to the arts. Fig. 4.1 represents the basic components in Kosslyn's cognitive picture theory (Tye, 43).

Are mental images pictorial? We are not able to speak of them as objects of weight or substance. Kosslyn has proposed a model that should be acceptable and understandable for those of us in the arts, even if not fully acceptable by some researchers in areas such as physics, engineering, and psychology. His conceptual model proposes that mental images are similar to displays on a cathode-ray tube screen attached to a computer generating the displays on the screen. The displays are generated from information stored in the computer's memory. This is a dynamic model: it allows for human ability "to imagine entirely novel scenes, or our ability to add to or alter features of images" (Tye, 34). There appears to be general agreement that the concept of mental images like photographs stored in memory, and retrieved as the imaging experience occurs (hence the naive term "photographic memory")

Fig. 4.1
Cognitive Picture Theory: Basic Components

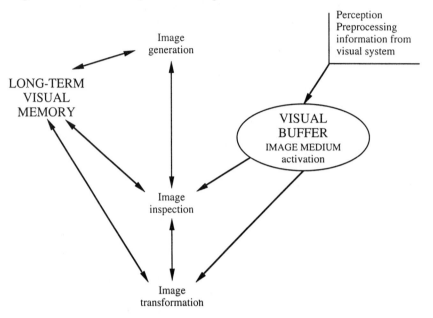

Processes that operate on images in the buffer:

generation: Appearances of objects and their spatial structure acts on informa-
                tion stored in long-term memory.

inspection: Recognizing shapes, spatial configurations, and the like, by examin-
                ing patterns of activated cells.

transformation: Processes that rotate, scale (proportionate size), or translate patterns
                of activated cells.

is not a logical explanation. Perhaps this is why no serious researcher or
scholar claims the existence of one hundred per cent eidetic imagery. We
should, however, be open to the realization of the limitless degrees of imagery, including eidetic, allowing for such an astounding mass of creativity and
critical thinking, array after array generated by the human mind, dynamic
not static, never one hundred per cent duplication.

     Michelangelo's marble figure of *Moses*, from the tomb of Pope Julius
II, serves well as an art object in our consideration of the cognitive picture
theory. There are at least two options of image medium: the marble statue,
itself, or a photograph of it. Most art critics and essayists describe this figure as possessing awesome strength and grandeur. Even with only the
photographic medium we are struck by the power in the figure. Those who
view and contemplate upon this *Moses* probably have no difficulty with agreement on the concept of power. However, if the reader will think back to the

Michelangelo Buonarroti. Head and torso of Moses, detail from the Tomb of Julius II. S. Pietro in Vincoli, Rome, Italy. B&W Print © 1998 Alinari/Art Resource, NY.

beginning of this chapter, he/she will recall the four questions. So, we can ask ourselves, "Can this image of power really exist in our minds?" Is it the same standoff between the descriptionalists and the pictorialists? The "power" image we find of *Moses* is not stored in our brains like a 35mm film or negative; we know that much. But it exists, ready for recall, whatever it is. We can describe it as the ineffable, a state of the aesthetic phenomena often encountered in the arts. Because of the conjunction of affective and cognitive

Fig. 4.2
Cognitive Picture Theory: Visual Buffer

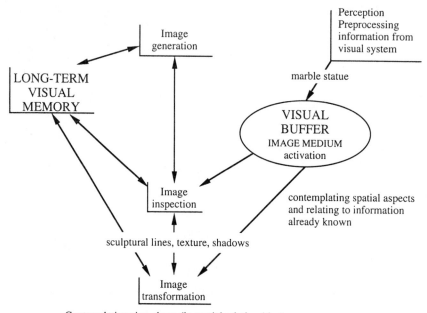

Contemplating size, shape (in spatial relationships)
light, changes of depth of texture

Image phase 1: Somatic perception: Vision. Brain receives information.

Image phase 2: Activation: Visual information. Brain holds initial marble image.

Image phase 3: Processing: a. Generation—spatial structure and other qualities of statue acts on long-term memory. b. Inspection—examines patterns of image (activated cells). c. Transformation—rotate, change, scale patterns down or up.

Image phase 4: Psychological perception, storage. In long term memory with reciprocal loading with the three processors. Phases 2, 3, and 4 are reciprocal and interactive. In this paradigm, areas of the brain most involved are: Limbic system—learning, memory, emotion, and monitoring from all sense organs; frontal lobes, sensory cortex, neocortex—learning and memory.

process, the mix of objective and subjective ideas one might find in any of
the arts, we should not be faulted for finding the term, "ineffable," so attractive. However, I submit that such aesthetic phenomena is not always
indescribable nor inexpressible. The mental associations of such words as
Michelangelo, Moses, marble sculpture, power, human and superhuman re-
solve, can contribute to certain mental images which could be frequently
recalled, post hoc. In most of the representations the head of Moses emits
two beams of light. In Michelangelo's rendition a pair of horns erupt from
the top front of the head. All other stories aside, it would seem that the horns
represent rays of light. Imagine how many students at this moment have a
very strong image of the *Moses*, because of the protuberances, specifically.

As we emphasize the aesthetic process of receiving (perceiving) as an
observer, we must consider another of the three faces of the aesthetic triad,
the process of creating. Michelangelo has given us cause to view his sculptures as noble and powerful. He often spoke of the human figure as the noblest
of all subjects. "And who is so barbarous as not to understand that the foot
of a man is nobler than his shoe" (Goldwater and Treves, 1972: 70).

In Figure 4.3 we see a four-phase image model as it applies to an auditory image, in this case a musical theme and variations played by a string
quartet. Phase 1 is somatic perception, specifically auditory. In this phase the
brain receives information. Phase 2 is one of activation, centered on audi-

Fig. 4.3
Cognitive Picture Theory: Auditory Buffer

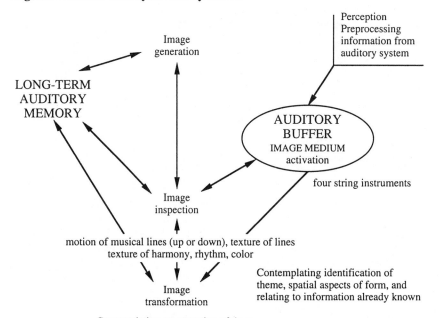

tory information. The brain holds initial temporal images such as a quartet of stringed instruments and obvious characteristics. Phase 3 is processing that consists of three different processors: generation—spatial structure and other qualities of sound acts on long-term memory; inspection—examines patterns of image (activated cells), tones up or down, fast, slow, loud, soft, etc.; and transformation—conserve audio: themes, rhythms, forms. Phase 4 is psychological perception: storage in long term memory with reciprocal loading with the three processors.

In this auditory example, phases 2, 3, and 4 are reciprocal and interactive. In the paradigm, areas of the brain most involved are: limbic system (learning), memory, emotion, and monitoring from all sense organs; frontal lobes, sensory cortex, neocortex (learning and memory).

In *The Imagery Debate* (1991), Michael Tye has devoted a substantial amount of space to explaining and verifying the empirical evidence which Kosslyn and his colleagues have gathered in support of Kosslyn's picture theory. Tye reports other process and evidence from nine different experiments (Tye, 33–60). The most important findings in the studies point to a general position which could be very meaningful in relation to all the arts: that vision (perception) and imagery share various inspection processes and the same medium (visual buffer).

IMAGES IN PROGRAM MUSIC

If the cognitive picture theory is compatible with the visual arts concepts and phenomena, it yet remains to state a case for the compatibility of the theory with musical arts concepts and phenomena. Earlier in this chapter, figure 4.3 presented a music model similar to the figure 4.2, which represented visual art in relation to the picture theory. Fortunately, we have available striking examples of music that bring into focus both auditory and visual phenomena in tandem, works that have been designated as "program music," or, in the eighteenth and nineteenth centuries, "programme music."

Imagination, Creativity, and Images in Program Music

Program music is musical sound used to depict objects or incidents which, themselves, are nonmusical or "extramusical" phenomena. This suggestion of a program or extramusical idea is not only found in the title of the composition, but is also found frequently in written remarks by the composer explaining the extramusical idea(s). In considering how emotion and meaning are inserted into music, we know that so much of that subject has been put into print over the years (most notably throughout the entire nineteenth century) by critics, essayists, and other literati, that aesthetic issues, themselves, become emotional, with objectivity often in decline.

Vestiges of nineteenth-century romanticism remain with us even in the late twentieth century. A part of that classic and romantic heritage was imbued with the rise of program music, music that was intended by the composer to represent something outside of itself: an extramusical idea. Literati, and sometimes musicians, also referred to it as the "poetic idea." The classification of program music, against the more esoteric explanations favored by some scholars, probably evolved simply. The British term, "programme," was, in the nineteenth century accepted throughout western Europe and the United States as interchangeable with the term "playbill," which might serve for opera, recital, play, vaudeville, and concert. For concerts, this became significant as composers of this kind of instrumental music actually described in their own words the extramusical ideas and meanings that inspired or suggested some general feelings, thoughts, and activity. These might fit into images to which the listener could associate if he or she had already received the descriptive rhetoric of the composer's creation which would appearing in the concert program.

Examples of program music date all the way back to the fourteenth century, with this music (mostly vocal forms) of Italy, France, and England actually describing in the text such things as street scenes, hunting scenes, birds, storms, and battles. These early examples of program music derived their descriptions from their text, not from musical sounds in themselves. From around 1350 to 1750, some keyboard music (harpsichord and virginal) included serious attempts to describe extramusical ideas and images solely through instrumental means.

By the beginning of the nineteenth century, the instrument families of the modern orchestra as we know it today were fully developed. With only modest improvements to the strings needed, it was for the wind instrument makers to bring each member in the brass, woodwind, and percussion families to the high levels of technical facility, endurance, and sound that nearly equals those instruments more than a century later. In particular, the improvements made with the flute (1825), clarinet (1825), oboe and bassoon (1850), French horn, trumpet, and tuba (1830) contributed to the romantic spirit of the time, to the opportunities for increased tone color, dramatic dynamic levels and change. These developments played a large role in some of the popularity of program music for the symphony orchestra

In 1808, Beethoven presented his Symphony no. 6, *Pastoral*. To most music historians, this marks the beginning of program music of the nineteenth century. Yet, "Beethoven affirmed that his Pastoral Symphony was an expression of emotion rather than tone-painting" (Harrison and Westrup, 1960). Willi Apel has stated that "this symphony is, no doubt, the greatest example—perhaps the only really great example—of program music" (Apel, 1956). The great lexicographer was probably a bit overzealous in his statement. We should keep in mind, however, that from approximately 1750 to 1850 there existed among the public, just as today, two tracks of musical interest, music as art and as entertainment: art music—that which holds its value in its own forms, making permanent human ideas and expression, reshaping nature, creative, and an adventure of the mind, contrasts with music as entertainment—that which arises from a more popular, banal, and populist vein, serving more transitory tastes and needs of the public. These two tracks coexisted, much as they do today. From all nineteenth-century accounts, program music appeared on stage in the concerts of the highest musical order, but also appeared in French opera comique, German *singspiel* and vaudeville (short comedies filled with popular songs which in earlier times were, themselves, called vaudevilles). Such music often served for presenting images of battles, danger, birds in song and flight, and most anything that might serve to imitate nature.

In early eighteenth-century France there was a reasonable consensus among critics and essayists that imitation of nature was the main objective of music. Composers and performers were less in agreement with that idea. However, at that time there were numerous examples of French harpsichord literature, and some violin literature, in which the composer attempted above all else to imitate nature, and those who chose not to imitate nature were criticized.

During the eighteenth century, both Haydn and Mozart contributed, among their monumental compositions, also works that would be considered something other than art music. For example, Haydn wrote popular comic opera and fragments, *burlettas* (among the most popular Italian forms of musical comedy at the time), and musical fragments for marionettes; and Mozart wrote numerous lesser-known fragments for *singspiel* (sung and spoken dialogue), not unlike nineteenth-century British vaudeville or twentieth-century American Broadway musicals, as well as comic vocal ensembles such as *Druck und Schluck*.

Both Mozart and Haydn had two mutual friends who were extremely important in the nineteenth-century world of European musical entertainment: Benedict Schack and Johann Schikaneder. Schack, a singer, composer, conductor, and creator of the role of "Tamino" in *The Magic Flute*, collaborated with Mozart to the extent that the authenticity of credits for some of their lighter comic pieces is not yet entirely clear between the two of them. Schikaneder, singer, librettist, theatre manager and director of a touring company, wrote the libretto for *The Magic Flute*. Mozart wrote numerous comic vocal solos and ensembles for the vaudeville-type touring company, many of which were not recognized beyond the theater's confines, and probably were lost or destroyed.

My intent here is not to belabor the concept of coexistent worlds of art music and musical entertainment, but rather to stress the perspective of a long-standing history (1350–1850) of program music, with its imitation of nature, its dealing with natural objects. Generated from popular entertainment, it sometimes found its way into more serious forms in the concert hall, evident in both tracks.

Early in the nineteenth century, Beethoven and Franz Schubert created for the concert hall works that would serve as harbingers of the new romanticism that would nourish the melding of literary ideas and music, Beethoven, with his *Pastoral* Symphony, and Schubert with his song cycle, *Die Schone Mullerin* (The Lovely Miller Maid).

Amid interest in the fusion of the arts was a particular emphasis upon the relationship between music and words. During the first half of the nineteenth century, many musicians and composers were interested in literature and literary expression, and many romantic poets and novelists wrote with great understanding about music . . . The relationship between music and words was nowhere more important than in Germany at this time. (Olson, 1981: 136)

This interest in the connection of literary idea and music is obvious in the Beethoven symphony. In contrast to the usual classic four-movement symphony model, this composition has five movements, each with a descriptive title:

First movement—"Pleasant feelings on arriving in the country"

Second movement—"Scene by the brook"

Third movement—"Merrymaking of the peasants"

Fourth movement—"Storm"

Fifth movement—"Thankful feelings after the storm"

This is the first full-scale program symphony in that the titles of the various movements allude to extramusical ideas. As Beethoven did not go beyond giving titles, however, we should probably not consider them as being of primary importance; instead we should be most concerned with how the composer used such things as melodic ideas, rhythm patterns, tone, and form.

Franz Schubert's *Die Schone Mullerin*, completed in 1823, consists of a series of twenty songs that form a very general and loose story extolling the beauty of the millermaid who is observed from afar. The mill wheel and the brook are in our minds constantly as Schubert uses the piano accompaniment to carry out musical lines that run on and on, bounce, sparkle, and spatter in tandem with the constant turning of the wheel and the rushing of the water. While both the Beethoven symphony and the Schubert song cycle are represented herein as beginnings of nineteenth century program music, neither qualifies as true romantic era program music. (We can remind ourselves that this in no way detracts from the value of these compositions as artistic masterpieces.) The symphony does not extend beyond the mere titling of the sections, and in the song cycle the only aspect of programmatic nature to deal with would be the piano accompaniment.

After Beethoven and Schubert, composers began to produce large-scale instrumental works bearing not only titles, but literary "programs" that described emotional impressions. Subjects of the compositions could be based on literary, or even pictorial, ideas. Composers supplied the verbal descriptions in concert programs to indicate to the listener the ideas that inspired the work. It is best that we not go beyond the composer's own intent in our association with extramusical ideas.

Since 1830 program music has included no vocal music; it is purely instrumental. The modern orchestra now has a multitude of color possibilities; the great variety of timbre among the instruments contributes to a broad and interesting palette of tone, which can stimulate, build, or augment images such as flight, reverie, joy, calm, stress, darkness, and brightness. Hector Berlioz (1803–1869) around 1830 completed in Paris his *Symphonie Fantastique* (Fantastic Symphony), which was created by adding to the romantic concept of literary program the principle of thematic unity in which some extramusical idea is represented by a melody or other musical idea. This melody Berlioz designated as a "fixed idea" (see illustration 4.2). In Berlioz's own words, the program consists of the dreams and feelings of a young musician-poet who has drugged himself with opium because of his unrequited love for a woman. The image of the woman becomes an obsession, represented by the fixed idea that appears throughout the work, often in a transformed or varied state (Olson, 1981: 198–200).

Even without knowing the program, we can enjoy and appreciate this sensational work. The symphonic treatment is of a high order. It is interesting to note that the first movement is in a sonata design: main theme—second theme—development of the main theme—recap of main and second themes. The movement has unity through the form produced by this thematic treatment. The entire symphony has unity because of the "fixed idea" (main theme) recurring in all the movements. This cyclical mode exists in the composition as an abstract musical phenomenon, as does the coexisting program in which the image of the "beloved" appears again and again in all of the movements.

Eidetic Imagery—More than Fantasy

From the previously discussed *Fantastic Symphony* by Berlioz we can move comfortably to a discussion of eidetic imagery. Although this work by Berlioz is considered the first true program composition (c. 1820), it might not inspire any more imagery than the earlier work, Symphony no. 6, the *Pastoral* Symphony, by Beethoven. The big difference here is the intent of the composer. Beethoven had little concern as to how well he had described scenes associated with the titles he assigned to each movement. By his own words, he was concerned about expressing his feelings through the sound and struc-

Ill. 4.2
Symphonie Fantastique: Idee Fixe

The symphony, in five movements, is designed as follows:
a. First movement-- "Reveries and Passions"

Berlioz' program presents the musician in a delirious state contemplating the intense love this woman has inspired in him. The fixed idea reappears frequently.

b. Second movement-- "A Ball"

At a ball, in the midst of festive and noisy dancing and conversation, he sees his beloved again.
   1) The fixed idea is now transformed into a lilting waltz figure.

c. Third movement-- "Scene in the Fields"

A peaceful summer evening in the country. His calm is broken by the reappearance of the beloved's image. The sun has set, and there is thunder in the distance.

d. Fourth movement-- "March to the Scaffold"

He dreams that he has killed his beloved, is condemned to death, and is led to the guillotine. He thinks of his beloved (a reappearance of the fixed idea) just before the fall of the blade.

e. Fifth movement-- "Witches' Sabbath"

He sees himself at a diabolical orgy for his burial. Now the beloved appears in transformation; her melody is now a vulgar witches' dance.

Hector Berlioz's "fixed idea" from the *Symphonie Fantastique*.

ture of his music; thus, there are no descriptive statements to accompany the titles. If the first-time listener were not given the titles of the movements, it would prove to be almost impossible, upon hearing, to identify by anything near the descriptions in the titles (e.g., second movement: "scene by the brook"). Berlioz, on the other hand, has played out a drama for us. His five movements are not only titled; they each become like a written-out descriptive episode in a five-part story, with some occasional extramusical detail or object vividly created temporally. A case in point is the fourth movement, "March to the Scaffold." In Berlioz's original program notes shown on the previous page, he reportedly refrained from including the literary depiction of the beheading of the hero. Yet, as we have a good idea of what the executions were like in Paris at the end of the eighteenth century, it is not difficult both to see and hear with the roll of the snare drum the guillotine blade ready to fall; then with the orchestra's downward accented crash, the blade completing its course; and finally, with the low bouncing pair of string pizzicato notes, the grotesque bounce of the hero's severed head into the basket below.

Despite all the intensity that Berlioz brought to the programmatic mode of his composition, without any knowledge of the program before or during the hearing, the uninitiated listener could not be expected to make any associations with even the most general ideas, such as those expressed in the movement titles (reveries and passions, a ball, scene in the fields, march to the scaffold, and witches sabbath), let alone some of the more specific programmatic content. However, familiarity with the program changes the mode of receiving completely: even without any familiarity with the music beforehand, but informed about the program, listeners are able to make intelligent associations with the events or objects represented in the composition. Thus, it is not surprising that the validity of most of the associations increases even more as the listener becomes more familiar with the music as it relates to the images triggered and sustained by the literary units.

In my teaching of music history, aesthetics, and introduction to music courses, as well as in related seminars and workshops over the period from 1961 to 1992, I developed a bias toward employing the literature of the mighty orchestra of the nineteenth and twentieth centuries whenever we reached those times in the course of study. Not that I gave short shrift to piano, vocal/choral, and opera literature; I simply found that I could stimulate more interest in the great literature of the classic, romantic, and modern eras by emphasizing the contrasts and similarities between the program works and the monumental abstract forms of the symphony. And, by 1979, I had become curious about the extent of imaging produced as a cognitive process by my students in the intro to music course as well as in music history courses.

During the twelve-year period 1979 to 1991, I developed the practice of selecting two or three of those courses per year as experimental groups, and inserting at the appropriate time in the course of study a brief nonassertive outline and specific discussion of four program compositions: *Symphonie Fantastique*, by Berlioz, *In the Steppes of Central Asia*, by Borodin, *The Moldau*, by Smetana, and *Don Juan*, by Richard Strauss. Occasionally, some alternates were substituted, such as *Scheherezade*, by Rimsky-Korsakov, and *Afternoon of a Faun*, by Debussy. The remainder of the intro to music and music history classes, the control groups, received much the same literature, of course, but without the benefit of the "treatment." After first hearing the compositions in class, we then directed our attention to the same information that the experimental groups had received before listening. Although this exercise was administrated as a controlled and consistent study, it existed as a qualitative evaluation study rather than as quantitative experimental research.

I relied upon feedback from the class for information and observation of each student's progress in the program music listening tasks. Students were aware that this activity had no bearing on class grade, except for possibly developing skills helpful in the final listening exam for the course. I considered this as a one-tailed (directional) study, with data collated as follows:

Qualitative Evaluation—Olson Students 1979–91 Period
Report on Assessment of Task, "Approach to Listening to Program Music,"
Unpublished study, Minnesota State University System, 1991

Number of Intro to Music and Music History students over period: 2300.

The largest class numbered 250, and the smallest class numbered nine. Total number of classes was fifty-three.

| Group A ("experimental") | Number selected: 17 | Number of students: 748 |
| Group B ("control") | Number selected: 15 | Number of students: 685 |

I persisted in using the labels "experimental" and "control" even though that might be stretching the nomenclature a bit, as I found the study easier to explain by including such wording. I selected the classes by randomization tempered by my schedule and other calendar considerations. Students had no choice in participation decision, thus I could be assured of as unbiased sampling as possible. The majority of the students were hardly aware of any research or experimentation in progress, as the study instruments and devices remained relevant to the outcomes of the course. Responses from only a relatively few students had to be discounted. These were mainly music majors in some of the music history classes, who had some time earlier been exposed to one or more of the six works. At least a few majors knew of some of that literature before entering college. On the more somber side, the nonmusic majors group, which comprised more than three-fourths of the subject pool, included only a few subjects with any prior experience of any of the six works.

Discussion and Conclusions. Group A classes were generally far ahead of Group B at the initial listening to the Berlioz, Borodin, Smetana, and Strauss. Group A's prepping allowed them to make associations between the music and the extramusical ideas. The two alternates, *Scheherezade* and *Don Juan*, proved to be a more difficult task for the groups for whom they were inserted, as the extramusical ideas were a bit more obscure. Such sections as "March to the Scaffold" in the Berlioz and "The Rapids" in the Smetana, were already very specific in the minds of Group A subjects, so that images were already forming.

Group B classes, with treatment withheld, had absolutely no idea of what the program might be at any points of any of the compositions presented in the initial listening session. For example, after hearing *The Moldau*, students would have no idea what the program might be even for the seventh section, the rapids. None of the subjects, at first hearing, could hook on to an image such as rapids or whitewater. However, a most important point must be emphasized here. The B classes, in fact, did experience some extremely valid images in conjunction with specific parts of the compositions. For example, the vast majority of each B class, in the initial hearing, would respond to the rapids, writing down such descriptors as "flowing," "crashing," "sweeping," "powerful," and "chaos." Some occasional use of metaphor would appear in these exercises. As the students were introduced to the program ideas of all four works, they found the meld of literary and musical ideas very logical and comfortable.

Both A and B groups received within their music library listening tapes and outlines some specific guides that—it is hoped—reinforced the programmatic images for the works in question. In the final exam, listening section, for the intro to music classes, there always appeared overwhelming evidence that the subjects were able greatly to increase their ability to develop both visual and auditory images. Such cognitive activity, exercises, seemed to contribute to the subjects' enjoyment, which led, in turn, to additional interest in such activity.

Creative/Critical Thinking and Eidetic Imagery

Experimental method in the area of eidetic imagery is, admittedly, imperfect science at this moment. Yet, it gives promise of contributing to the body of new information on cognition and human behavior. As part of a presentation, "Music, Critical Thinking, and Reform" at the Music Educators National Conference, National Biennial, at Kansas City, Missouri, on April 18, 1996, I included a report from my ongoing arts and imagery research. A brief summary follows:

Cognitive Events Referenced to Stimuli Produced by Specific Music Listening Experiences

Complex musical events, all of which involve critical thinking, can be divided into three classifications: creating, performing, and receiving (listening). All involve certain degrees of critical thinking. Over the past several decades the increased emphasis on cognitive processes in music listening, as well as performance and composing has led some psychologists and music researchers to attach much more significance to the musical experience as an important part of human perception and learning.

Study of the "miracle" of eidetic imagery as aesthetic function and as phenomena finds its way to the arts through both psychology and philosophy. Earlier research and pertinent literature emphasized eidetic imagery as not generally related to memory ability itself, but an isolated curiosity. However, current research in the cognitive sciences has increased in the area of imagery, with many new texts which include the subject.

Tye (1991) has presented ideas of a broad spectrum of psychologists who over the years have been interested in the role of mental images in human cognition. From a large body of experimental data two general theory groups have developed: mental images as pictures, and mental images as linguistic description.

The current studies involving metacognition or "higher order" thinking offer a solid approach to the tandem of arts—creativity—critical thinking. Studies and compilations by Bruner (1957), Pflederer (1967), and Sternberg (1988) contributed greatly to an emphasis on concepts of conservation, form, and relationships, and various strong developmental paradigms for the arts.

If we approach eidetic imagery as both a critical thinking process and a creative process, we can, with some assurance, relate it to cognitive effects of certain listening experiences.

Objectives of the study were as follows: (1) to determine the presence or absence of eidetic imaging in context with specific music examples on the part of the subjects; (2) to determine if such imaging can be enhanced by cognitive reinforcement; and (3) to investigate the possible role that perceptual style might play in the processes of eidetic-like imagery related to musical sound stimuli.

Experimental design. A single-subject ABAB design was used. This simple but extremely reliable, two-part design is in reality a four-phase design: initial period of baseline observations; initial introduction of the treatment variable; withdrawal of the treatment variable (second baseline); and reintroduction of the treatment variable.

Method. Six subjects received the *Witkin Embedded Figures Test* (Witkin, 1971) as an antecedent measurement variable one week before the administration of the experiment. The subjects participated in the experiment, two at a time. Experiment time was fifty-five minutes and progressed as follows: the first phase (A), as a baseline condition, progressed to the second phase (B), as the treatment condition in which a reinforcement contingency was established. In the third phase the treatment condition was removed, resulting in a return to baseline conditions (A). The experiment ended with a reintroduction of the treatment variable (B). Schema= A1—B1—A2—B2. The Inventory was given at the end of each of the four phases.

Materials. Cassette containing specific portions of *The Moldau* by Smetana, *In the Steppes of Central Asia* by Borodin, and *Clouds* by Debussy. Additional materials included a set of selected illustrations and cue cards (Treatment Materials), an audio cassette tape player, a set of *Witkin Group Embedded Figures Test* copies (Antecedent Variable), and the *Program Music Images Inventory.*

Results. Subjects varied significantly in their ability to obtain and retain "mental pictures" in context with the listening tasks; the immediate learning environment, particularly the treatment phase, appeared to influence most heavily the ability to image through associations "triggered" by cues such as castles or shimmering. The field-independent subjects did slightly better in obtaining and retaining the images. The subjects' musical background seemed to have little effect on the task.

ICONS AND IMAGES

Suzanne Langer (1957) is among the first of modern philosophers to consider present data and conceptual forms that can be applied directly to arts, critical thinking, and the aesthetic transaction. In her writings, she emphasizes the basic importance—or better put, basic need—of three phenomena: (a) significant form, (b) real, or factual meaning in art, and (c) symbolism and its power in regard to intellectual excitement.

Langer articulated concepts and percepts that today remain as primal among the community of philosopher-aestheticians. Much of the research during the infancy of experimental aesthetics has relied upon Langer's "keystone ideas" dealing with her "fabric of meaning" and the important relationship among the three modes of the arts: creative, productive, and receptive.

Today, with immense help from the neurosciences, we carry on some of Langer's ideas with research in the filtering and manipulating of sensory input as it applies specifically to attention, centration, and metacognition, and what has now returned to the concepts of the "image."

Image and Environment

In the creation of a work of art, man engages in a struggle with nature not for his physical but for his mental existence.

(Conrad Fiedler, 1949: 48)

To Conrad Fiedler the arts and philosophy are alike in that both are cognitive in their main effort to become a continuous, incessant working of the mind to bring one's consciousness of the visible world to an ever richer development. Herbert Read recognized the importance of aesthetic awareness as a human function. Like Fiedler, he considered the arts as the means by which humankind can comprehend the nature of things; it is the piecemeal recognition and fixation of what is significant in human experience.

In *Icon and Idea* (1965), Read considers the important role of visual art as a constant factor all the way back to the dawn of human culture and continuously up to the present time. He reminds us that art has surely remained a key to survival. Most relevant to discussion of image, however, is his proposition that since the time of the Sumerians, art objects have given evidence of man's awareness of symmetry and balance, the two most obvious organic qualities of an art object. In relating images and qualities, however, Read proposes that prehistoric man sought out artistic activity as a combination of ritual, superstition, storytelling, primitive recording, and aesthetic expression/

reflection. His proposals remain very much in tune with writings of many of the outstanding anthropologists of this past century. To him, the high quality of certain examples of prehistoric art existed because of a kind of dual-center, a center or focus on vitality, and another on beauty. The unbroken line of "cultural activity" for five millennia has continued, driven by this need for the human mind to manipulate and refashion its world. At the end of our twentieth century, this ineffable drive still leads us to realize outwardly the image, and feel inwardly the sensation. Although today we might be reflecting more on process and phenomena, able to discuss complex neurological effect involved in various arts activities, we are probably still invoking the same basic "cultural activity" as humans did thousands of years ago.

Daniel C. Dennett (1981) has pointedly described mental imagery as a myth that is "beginning to lose its grip on thinkers in the field." Unfortunately, Dennett expects far too much of the concept of mental imagery. Citing a "wealth of cross-disciplinary confusions over mental images," he might have added to the confusion, himself. Veteran scholars from the fields of psychology, neurosciences, philosophy (including aesthetics), and more recently, some specific arts areas have continued to demonstrate curiosity and concern for the recognition of imaging as a general cognitive function that could at any moment depend upon, or work toward, such conditions as creativity, critical thinking, or simply involuntary retinal stimulation and response to the subject's visual environment.

From the standpoint of the philosopher and artist, Dennett, with his bias toward descriptive accounting (as opposed to pictorial), has failed to bring about any useful definitions or theorems that apply particularly to creative thinking. And, more unfortunately, he has completely neglected the imaginative/creative aspects of imaging. It is not by accident that individuals identified as "creative" report or display a tendency to employ both pictorial and descriptive processes. Most scholars, even when approaching the most exalted of all imagery, eidetic memory, do not accept the eidetic phenomenon as final, static, homeostatic. In such eidetic memory images, the "picture in the mind's eye" is not always one superimposed on the subject's visual field, fixed, moving with the eye as afferent (leading inward to a central organ or nerve). Is there anyone today who claims the existence of a one hundred percent eidetic or a "photographic" memory? Have any of us experienced, or known of, even one example of an eidetic phenomenon in which a mental picture is recalled through afferent processes and superimposed on incoming neural stimulation, to the extent that every minute detail in that picture is still there? Is not an afferent neural process in this case an involuntary one?

These aspects of the involuntary physiological processes of perception must remain different from those creative, causal, and imaginary psychological processes in which the subject builds, creates, imagines, and analyzes within the boundaries of reason, often as one who desires to "play with and sometimes mentally modify the natural scene." All painters, poets, sculptors, composers, and choreographers do it. It should be emphasized here that this mental playing or exercising over the natural scene has little or nothing to do with the concept of hallucination, which is involuntary, uncontrolled, and probably void of any productive process. (Neuroscientists seem to be in agreement that hallucinations are caused by abnormal discharges of neurons.) Creative imagination has nothing to do with hallucinations; while the latter are involuntary processes, the former can be overtly and covertly created, developed, stored in short-term or long-term memory; they can be used or reused on call, in associations, or discretely, for action-taking as well as pondering or reflecting upon.

Those who insist that imaging is more like depicting in words than painting a picture, seem to ignore the broad spectrum of controlled imagination found among any literate population. In the steady growth of cognitive studies and such specific areas as experimental aesthetics, it is not very difficult to find evidence, or at least predictive observations, of processes which can now be found in some cognitive psychology literature under the heading of "imagistic representation."

Imagistic Representation

Some cognitive scientists acknowledge the existence and importance of images in cognitive processes. Yet, they make strong statements against the idea that thinking might consist of imaging. They also emphasize that image and symbol are very different. These ideas do not cause any discomfort among artists, musicians, or even poets. They lead toward the aesthetic concepts that many of us embrace, concepts that become syndromic, a melding of many varieties of representations—image, symbol (even icon) at any given moment—as well as nonrepresentations—specific forms that arise from an intense need for logic and balance. Thus, the creative inner voice is constantly at work, receiving or "causing."

Images, Creativity, and Memory

In considering creativity in the arts, we might focus on an issue that has been the subject of experimentation and modeling: if images can be generated by the mind, is that generation really only a retrieval of pieces of stored information, or is it a melding of units that have been stored separately? (Kosslyn, et al., 1981). A corollary might well be added by seeking to find if the images, complexity and intensity considered, were, in fact, pictorial or only descriptive or both.

I do not believe that we can overstate the importance of the arts as adventures of the mind. Those adventures, however, are fueled by images. We cannot think of cognitive activity that embodies such constructs as ideas, feelings, impressions, expressions, and attention, without relating to "image" and "imaging." Kaelin (1989) cites the philosopher Benedetto Croce as author of numerous idealistic concepts in which separation of artifact from the "work of art" communicates original ideas of the artist and subsequent values through expression or embodiment of feelings. Croce states that the artist creates his expressions by painting or sculpting, by writing or composing, thereby presenting something that is capable of being "physically beautiful." However, Croce adds, " the artist never in reality makes a stroke with his brush without having previously seen it with his imagination" (quoted in Kaelin, 40). At the turn of the century and as the first half of the twentieth century played out, the idealism of scholars such as Croce became surrounded by the new ideas of philosophers such as Edmund Husserl, the founder of phenomenology, a system which grew mainly out of attempts to offer descriptive schema and studies of the constructs of consciousness. Most closely related to the arts were his attempts to systematically describe "consciousness" in order to differentiate between laws of objective experience and those of pure imagination. To Husserl, consciousness does not exist apart from the objects to which it attends.

As interest in phenomenological aesthetics has, since the turn of the century, increased to the status of a full-fledged area of study within the field of philosophy, its questions, answers, models, hypotheses, and insinuations have found their ways into a broad and varied range of academic endeavors. Works of Husserl, Heidegger, and Sartre have helped to stoke fires of interest which have spread to areas of "pop" philosophy, contributing to the unleashing of the ponderous force of "isms" now embedded in twentieth-century thought: for example, relativism, postmodernism, dynamism, neoabsolutism, perspectivism, and many others.

5

Arts, Aesthetics, and the Umbrella of Critical Thinking

In *On Judging Works of Visual Art* (1949: 53) Conrad Fiedler suggested that a likeness appears between art and philosophy in that both are cognitive in their main effort to become a continuous, incessant working of the mind to bring one's consciousness of the visible world to an ever richer development. This continuous, incessant process is a good starting point for us in any attempt to define critical thinking.

Critical thinking denotes disciplined processes of analyzing, synthesizing, or evaluating information resulting from observation, reasoning, or reflection based upon intellectual values that apply to all areas of human experience. If present trends continue, schools in the near future will be evaluating programs more on objective performance-based criteria. This will affect more than social studies, math and science, and English; it will have impact upon all the arts.

Like the other arts, music is closely tied to aesthetic experience and critical thinking. Carl Gustav Jung, the founder of analytical psychology, relied upon relationships between aesthetic perception and various cognitive conditions in developing or explaining certain behavioral models and theories. What makes the arts so enjoyable, so vital, in our lives is the constant mingling of the cognitive (the thinking) with the affective or emotional conditions. If we can agree that music at its highest order of thinking involves an intense cognitive process, that is, nevertheless, joined by sometimes strong affective (feeling, emotional) processes, then we can think of this union of the logical and the emotional, the objective and the subjective, as probably the reason why we have such deep feelings for some of our music.

THE ARTS: A BLOSSOMING OF THE HUMAN MIND

It might be of value to begin a discussion of the nature of music, not with a musician, but rather with a philosopher. In the final analysis, music is a matter of the mind, and Arthur Schopenhauer (1788–1860), a German philosopher, had some profound things to say about music as an art—statements that remain valid to this day. Schopenhauer referred to art as the "flower of life," a level of experience to which individuals can rise, and in which there can be a temporary release from individuality. To Schopenhauer, music appeared to be the highest of the arts, reflecting human life at its three basic stages: struggle or striving, temporary satisfaction, and satiation and boredom.

When an individual listens to a piece of music, does that person hear all there is to hear? Can one be aware that even some of the simple "pop" melodies or folk tunes have form similar to melodies found in works regarded as monuments of music? If we are perceptive, we can often find similarities among many different kinds of music. This perceptiveness opens up broader areas of understanding and enjoyment.

It seems reasonable to believe that the individual who enjoys examples of popular music, as well as opera and concert music, will certainly have more opportunities for enjoyment than one who enjoys only one kind of music. It also seems reasonable that we might better understand and enjoy music if we consider it in its relationships with the other arts, as well as to consider it within its own limits and peculiarities.

What Is Art?

What Art Is	What Art Is Not
a reflection of human ideas	a series of mere facts
expression made permanent	permanent objects without expression
an adventure of the mind	something from which all minds obtain the same stimuli
artificial	practical and useful in satisfying basic needs in everyday life
creative and free	bound by moral, ethical, and social codes
a reshaping of nature	nature itself
evokes ideas bringing about enjoyment or displeasure	something that offers pleasure in itself

Different people have different ideas of what art really is. Most, however, find it difficult to describe or define it. The following ideas might help the reader to form his own definition: (1) Art has to do with mind; it is intelligence playing over a natural scene; (2) It is personal expression made permanent; the painter puts his ideas onto canvas; the sculptor his ideas into wood, bronze, or plaster; the composer or poet his ideas into symbols which will later be translated into sound. All have created something available for others as well as himself to perceive and reflect upon at future moments; and third, the composer, writer, painter, sculptor, or architect has created something and made certain arrangements of shape, size, mass, time, sound, or color in a manner satisfying to himself or herself.

Art, in all forms, is undoubtedly the most certain kind of expression for humankind. Ever since the beginning of history, men and women have made things for their use and things necessary for their existence. They have created languages and symbols and various inventions in an unceasing progression in search of material happiness. Yet, there has always been a feeling in every historical period that this material searching alone is inadequate. While the scientific searching is satisfied with concrete, objective facts, beyond this objectivity there is an aspect which is reached only through instinct and intuition. The purpose of art is to develop these more obscure methods of understanding. To understand humankind, we must realize the significance of knowledge that is embodied in art.

Art and Beauty

It is far too simple to say that art and beauty are the same. Indeed, art is often concerned with the expression of feelings of beauty, but it can also be to some an expression of the grotesque or ugly. People have embraced through the arts different ideas of beauty or value throughout various historical periods. For example, the ancient Greeks expressed a love of splendor and order; medieval man expressed a deep religious and superstitious nature; Renaissance man seemed to display a desire for freedom, secularism, material comforts or interests, as well as "classic beauty." Art works of other periods likewise reflect the temper of the times. One might see in paintings and sculpture of the seventeenth century a beauty often expressed with more emotional power and decoration than in previous periods. Maybe that is why musical drama, the opera and oratorio, developed and flourished so much at that time. The arts during the eighteenth century, with their emphasis upon clarity, reason, and the "gallant" style; the arts during the nineteenth century, with their nationalism; and twentieth-century art with its dissonances and technology—all identify with their own times. This identification is a process repeated over and over again throughout the centuries, the process of creating art through which the composers or painters or writers are able to fill expressive needs peculiar to them and their own environments.

Comparing the Arts as Means of Expression

If we accept the ideas of "what is art" thus far presented in this chapter, then it remains for us to determine how the various arts convey ideas. No two arts express in the same way. Each art has a responsibility, naturally imposed, to express in its own manner, as is described below:

Music: Sound is the medium. It is temporal, thus requires memory.

Painting: Pigments, canvas, paper, etc., serve as the medium. It can be representational (illustrating an object as it appears naturally), or it can be abstract (presenting ideas, expressions or impressions which have been stimulated by an object).

Sculpture: Stone, clay, wood, and metals serve as the mediums. It imitates nature. One might look upon a piece of sculpture as motion in a frozen form (mobiles and kinetic sculpture are exceptions).

Poetry: Word-symbols are the medium. It deals with ideas. However, poetry is often similar to music when it relies upon sound, and can become rhythmic or "musical." Poetry is the only one of the arts that has two such distinct facets: when read, it is closer to literature; when recited or read aloud, it is closer to music.

Literature: Word-symbols are the medium. It requires memory.

Dance: Freest of all arts. It would be most difficult to define or describe the medium, other than to say that it is the human body.

Architecture: The only one of the arts that can be totally functional. Emphasis is upon both a structural beauty and usefulness derived mainly from unity, variety, and balance.

At this point it might be worthwhile to momentarily bring together certain aspects of aesthetic phenomena, for as we continue to compare the various arts in respect to process, medium, and thought, we incessantly rely upon universal concepts which underpin all of our aesthetic experiences. In this chapter we have already begun to draw together the questions of identity of the arts, comparisons, and reasons for their being. Specific examples often give evidence that critical thinking, with its embedded processes and handling of information, is essential and unavoidable in such experiences.

The Cathedral Santiago de Compostela, Spain (shown in illustration 5.1) emphasizes this search for aesthetic satisfaction so often found over the ages throughout all the world.

Here is a cathedral built originally in the year 1130 in the typical pure Romanesque style. However, the west facade, as depicted herein, was added during the period 1738–50. This west front remains one of the most powerful examples of Baroque architecture standing. This facade, built over twelve years for purely ornamental purposes, is one of the great monuments to the human need for expression through art.

Ill. 5.1
Cathedral Santiago de Compostela

The Cathedral Santiago de Compostela (Spain), begun in 1130. The Baroque west front (1738–1750). Ink drawing, Gary Olson. Reproduced by permission of Gary Olson.

Music and Poetry: Temporal Aspects

As music and poetry both can have temporal qualities at any given moment, they present an obvious, but fascinating, similarity. When music is performed or poetry read aloud, either offer a dilemma of "Now you hear it, now you don't." Of all the other arts, only dance approaches the same dilemma. Dance might inspire us to remark, "Now you see and hear it, now you don't." However, the visual aspect of dance is so basic and necessary to the art itself that it might be considered more akin to the plastic arts, those that are more static, more permanent to the eye and mind.

Until the twentieth century, poets explored their medium only to the boundaries of "word pictures." In recent decades, poets have stretched the limits of poetry by producing works that are not primarily designed to convey specific ideas or word pictures, but, rather, are works designed to produce certain sound patterns and effects. In such a way, modern poets, such as Ezra Pound, e. e. cummings, and W. H. Auden, have pushed poetry more into the domain of music.

Comparing Music to More Static Forms: Sculpture

Some terms to define and clarify:

Static: At rest, not in motion.

Temporal: In motion, never at a point of static rest, with no permanent, "touchable" qualities.

Nonrepresentational: Qualities in, and of, any attempt to portray an object without inclusion of its most basic, obvious, or significant characteristics, or at least an attempt to obscure or rearrange some of them.

Abstract: A condition in which the qualities of an object have been removed and considered as entities in themselves—not specifics, but rather generalities; the opposite of the term "concrete." The color red is more abstract; a red rose is a more concrete idea.

If we agree with the definitions given above, we come to the realization that music is a temporal art, reliant upon tonal memory and imagery. This realization seems to demand a comparison of music with the more static or "plastic" forms that can rely upon more tangible attributes.

In comparing music with sculpture, some benign confusion arises: first, while sculpture is the most static of the arts, it often creates the illusion of time and movement as demonstrated in an example of classic Greek sculpture such as the *Discobolus* (discus thrower), in which motion is implied. Second, when static art is arranged for nonrepresentation—a nonrealistic portrayal of a natural object—it becomes abstract; it has meaning only in itself through what the beholder perceives in it. As an example, consider the bird as an art object in modern civilization. Indeed, for many centuries, artists and sculptors have attempted to re-create the figure of the bird as realistically as possible; they have tried to imitate nature. By the end of the nineteenth century, as abstraction entered into the visual arts, the bird as an object might be presented not only as the naturalist James Audubon (d. 1851) had done, but also as Constantin Brancusi did later with his work *Bird in Space* (1928) (see illustration 5.2), bringing abstraction to something that normally would not be abstract, but representative and very realistic.

Audubon combined keen perception with great craftsmanship to present civilization with an objective, near-to-nature visual record of various varieties of birds. On the other hand, Brancusi, through his abstract sculpture, stripped the bird of the very things that are so pointed and clear in Audubon's works: the colors, the realistically presented feathers and down, and the sensual aspects of texture of the entire object. He has left most to the imagination. As long as the viewer knows the title of the work as attached by the artist, he can certainly obtain ideas of expressive quality about the object. The ideas that the title, *Bird in Space* evokes in the viewer's mind might determine how he or she views it. The sleek, polished bronze missilelike form might bring to mind a powerful elongated bird soaring upward. The possibilities of associations are endless, differing to some extent with each viewer. Some viewers might refuse to recognize *Bird in Space* as a bird at all. As Brancusi has removed all representative qualities in making it abstract, he has cut off meaning of form from the object and has perhaps made a new form. Thus, as abstract art, it depends upon some verbal clue for its full effect; or otherwise the viewer will simply use his or her own imagination exclusively.

I am convinced that of all the arts, music presents the most opportunities for identifying all concepts that result from what I consider to be foundational (universal) bases of aesthetic phenomena. Concepts of process or phenomena, such as creativity, critical thinking, novelty, repetition, variation, form, conservation, divergence, convergence, variance, and invariance, are found in the six musical examples appearing later in this chapter and in more detail in chapter six.

Concluding our ruminations on the sculpture, *Bird in Space*, we might ready ourselves for the task of simultaneously considering the six musical examples, and treating them as unrelentingly related to the examples of sculpture and architecture offered in this text. We can then continue on with further emphasis on critical thinking in the arts with some very specific reference to the research of Jean Piaget, whose developmental approaches to learning and teaching fall nicely into line with the development of any and all aesthetic focus and discovery.

Ill 5.2
Bird in Space

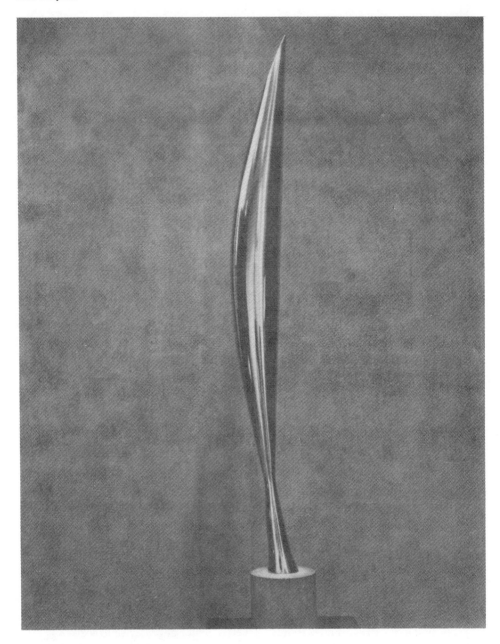

BRANCUSI, Constantin. *Bird in Space*. (1928) Bronze (unique cast), 54 x 8½ x 6½" (137.2 x 21.6 x 16.5 cm). The Museum of Modern Art, New York. Given anonymously. Photograph © 1998 The Museum of Modern Art, New York.

MUSIC LISTENING AND ANALYSIS: CRITICAL THINKING

Creativity and critical thinking are not discrete processes; both concepts seem to have ingress into all areas and levels of aesthetics and cognitive processes. In music, both rely on "conservation." The tasks to be performed in the following examples will involve conservation in which the music is constantly changing, and yet where there exists an invariance or changeless dimension throughout the performance. This conservation will be realized through creative and critical thinking. These musical examples briefly outlined for illustration have been chosen for the different approaches available within them to musical discovery and mastery of meaningful listening techniques. Examples 2–6 below appear in more detail in chapter six.

1. *Coventry Carol* (performed by the Canadian Brass [RCA ark 1-4132])
   a. a very old, familiar carol
   b. What happens in the third section?
   c. After hearing in the original form, we hear the original theme with variations.

2. *Camptown Races* (Dave Brubeck [Columbia CS 9284])
   a. old, popular Stephen Foster song
   b. What is "third-stream jazz"?
   c. How is this similar to the first example?

3. *Yesterday?* By Chopin? (*Glorieux Plays the Beatles* [Vanguard S 31-6410])
   a. Is this piece really by Chopin?
   b. What does it mean to be "in the style of Chopin"?

4. Mozart or *Mo's Art?* (Free Flight: *Slice of Life* [CBS FMT 44515])
   a. adaptation of the venerable C major Sonata, K.545

5. *Ladysmith Black Mambazo* (Shanachie 64053)
   a. African with western influences: diatonic scales, harmony
   b. How is repetition used?
   c. Although we cannot understand the language, can we understand the melodies, themselves? Why?

6. *My Melancholy Baby* (*Phil Mattson: Jubilee* [Doctor Jazz FW 40527])
   a. Is this improvisation? Variations?

The materials and methods employed in the previous section give us some opportunity to identify various aesthetic conditions or qualities that will be the object of critical thinking at various levels or phases—repetition, contrast, balance, variety, novelty—and also aesthetic supraconditions at various phases—generalization, improvisation, variation, and conservation. And, if we believe that this kind of discussion is becoming too prolix, too full of "isms" and "tions," too much an academic foofaraw, we might remind ourselves that since the time of Carl Gustav Jung (the founder of analytical psychology) practitioners and scholars in neurosciences and psychiatry have included the aesthetic process or transaction as part of human behavior, an essential ingredient in human cognition. When Jung in some of his writings referred specifically to aesthetics, he did so mainly in reference to perception, image processing and, not surprisingly, what we refer to as imagination. This cognitive process of imagination extends beyond subjective thought and feelings, beyond instinct; it involves what we have defined as critical thinking. If we are advocating, for the future, music as an equal partner in the curriculum, a partner in the learning core, involved in analysis, synthesis, interpretation, and thoughtful communication of ideas and feelings, then we will need to develop the programs that will indeed immerse students in activities that invoke such ideas and conditions.

Pflederer on Piaget's Conservation

The research of Swiss psychologist Jean Piaget (1896–1980) has indirectly exerted a great deal of influence on arts educators in terms of curriculum and application of thought processes. Piaget's studies in cognition and intellectual development in genetically determined stages continues to stimulate related study and research in the arts and sciences (Piaget, 1965). From the arts world, music educators led the way for more than three decades with particular interest in the developmental issues of "learning—retaining—using" concepts of Piaget that were nested in his developmental spiral as it pertains to five stages of childhood and adolescence:

Sensori-motor: Birth to 2 years
    congenital reflexes, neonate action patterns
    discoveries, actions and reactions centered on self

Pre-conceptual: Ages 2–4 years
    focus on own body to relate to environment
    thinking very singular

Intuitive (pre-operational): Ages 4–8 years
    perceptual dominance
    exogenous thinking

Operative: Ages 7–11 years
    grouping of concepts
    internalized actions

Formal-Operative: Ages 12–15 years
    use of hypothetical thinking
    deductive processes
    use of methodical and logical thought can now begin with
        theory, then verify relationships

Ages 2–8: reality, then theory. Ages 8–15: theory, then reality.

From ages eight to fifteen, when humans begin to group concepts to use as systems of action, and then connect theory with reality, the conservation principle becomes central to any consideration of critical thinking as a pro-

cess. Some powerful connections exist specifically between the arts and conservation. With the rich lodes of temporal, spatial, memory, and image tasks
found in music, dance, visual arts, poetry, and drama, it is no surprise that
investigations in those areas develop at the theoretical, empirical, and metaphorical levels.

Marilyn Pflederer (1964) was particularly successful in emphasizing the
connection of music learning with other kinds of learning, closely observing
the developmental patterns, and focusing on the embodiment of the Piagetian
principles of conservation. In her study, Pflederer concerned herself with the
rational aspects of musical development consisting of Piaget's operational
controls of concepts such as quantity, weight, volume, and class. She approached the problem of applying Piaget's principles to the development of
musical thought as follows:

The essence of musical intelligence is the building of a stable framework of rhythmic, melodic, harmonic, and formal concepts through a progressive organization of
musical experiences. It is this conceptual musical framework that permits individuals to reason about music. (Pflederer, 255)

Pflederer asserted that children and adults listen to music in temporal
sequence, constantly following tonal patterns as they occur. The listener con-
serves to various degrees any regular recurrent rhythm patterns. This he or
she does even when changes occur in the spatial melodic movement. This
kind of conservation gives us a clear-cut example of critical thinking, or
"higher thinking" in the arts. This ability to conserve such spatial melodic
movement, the kind of movement that might inspire us to describe and sculpt
with our hands in the air a melodic line we are hearing, should be a focal
point in any discussion of musical learning. The ability to conserve such
movement provides us with "a forward-moving scheme of expectation that
enhances both musical responsiveness and intellectual understanding of the
music" (Pflederer, 255).

As a superior form of mental organization, musical intelligence plays over
a mental "scene" in which the musical elements are the building blocks going into cognitive structures that are real, and that can be called up, or recalled,
through conservation. Even though the monumental works of composers such
as Mozart and Bach carry with them such quantities of ineffable affect and
cognition, such depths of development and mental exercise and adventure,
the works are indeed real; they were built, just as the ceiling paintings of
the Sistine Chapel were built.

Critical Thinking and the Aesthetic Transaction

I have occasionally interjected aspects of perceptual style under the topic
of cognitive style because of its immediacy to learning in the arts as well as

other areas of human experience. Consider the following group of human be-
haviors and characteristics, and reflect upon the importance of cognitive style
development as it might relate to aesthetic awareness:

Perceiving:
    wholeness in an artwork
    vital details
    "appearance" vis-a-vis medium
    form and shape
    global vs. specific

Realization that:
    Art has to do with the mind.
    It is intelligence playing over a natural scene.
    It is personal expression made permanent.
    It is something the creator makes available for others as well as
       himself/herself to perceive and reflect upon at future moments.

Receiving and understanding of art objects depends on the degree of development of perceptual styles and processing of background, forms, design,
and other insights in order to determine the certain phenomena that make up
the "essence" of an artwork: static or temporal state, representational or nonrepresentational, abstract or concrete.

AESTHETICS, EVERYDAY LIFE, AND MODERNISM

> Art, in its nobler acceptation, is an achievement, not an indulgence. It pre-
> pares the world in some sense to receive the soul, and the soul to master
> the world; it disentangles those threads in each that can be woven into the
> other.
>
> (George Santayana, 1953: 529)

The early pages of this chapter have been devoted to defining, comparing, and codifying the arts; the middle pages devoted mainly to drawing in
concepts of critical thinking and aesthetic awareness as they enmesh and suggest approaches to increased awareness. It remains to bring this chapter to a
close with a necessary inclusion of more problematic aspects: issues that are
no less vital aesthetically, yet are more mundane, more of what television
journalists refer to as "reality check" material. As a result, much of the last
third of the chapter is devoted to social, educational, and education reform
and the arts.

Maxine Greene: Arts and Social Issues

Maxine Greene, a renowned member of the faculty of Teachers College
of Columbia University, avers that she would consistently include in an arts

and humanities program certain works of history that promote awareness as well as meaning. She speaks of works that provoke "wide-awakeness." She would exclude "mathematized" or computerized history. For the other areas she would also strive to engage people in posing questions with respect to their own projects. She emphasizes the need in curriculum development to emphasize the task of clarifying, leaving no mysteries, no vagueness. She emphasizes the requirements of "making sense in a confusing world." She believes in the need and feasibility of interdisciplinary studies. To Greene, the arts are essential. Persons involved in the arts have "vantage" points for realizing their personal freedom. She believes that all the arts liberate those who come attentively to them. The arts "permit confrontations with the world as individuals are conscious of it, personally conscious, apart from 'the Crowd'" (Greene, 1978: 161–66).

Greene speaks of teachers and their need to be sensitive to art, in order to lead their students toward the arts. The new possibilities of vision and awareness available to students and teachers alike become reality wherever the curriculum allows and encourages the imaginative mode of awareness.

Ralph A. Smith and Percipience

On major U.S. college campuses today, if you were to ask the average student, possibly a member of a fraternity or sorority, what he or she thought of the Greek ideal as it relates to education in the modern world, you just might receive a vacant stare or an answer in which he or she related such an ideal to some panhellenic council activity on campus. You would realize that you were talking to a sensible person, yet one who had not the faintest idea of the Greek foundations of Western Civilization. Why? There continue to be frequent assaults on academic traditions, some subtle, some flagrant. This is apparent even in the areas of education where all share elements of a common heritage, some of those significant ideas which form the global spine of an evolving sense of discovery and learning. Some people like it that way. In their sometimes benighted ways of thinking, they would like to erase all historical connections with ancient Greek traditions, striking a blow for whatever agenda their new age, "postmodern" credo seems to demand. Indeed, there are noted scholars who think that much of the traditional cultural heritage is no longer relevant and stigmatize it by saying it is excessively Eurocentric. Yet as the terms of new "isms" creep into daily conversation, for example, neo-Marxism, contextualism, relativism, postmodernism, etc., there are writers, Ralph A. Smith among them, who recall the Greek ideal of excellence and its continuing relevance, a basic theme of his *Excellence in Art Education* (1987) and *Excellence II* (1995).

Smith, who has authored and edited several books and numerous articles on aesthetic education and served as editor of the *Journal of Aesthetic Education* since its inception, has been adept in analyzing trends in culture and aesthetic education. In his *The Sense of Art* (1989), his major statement on aesthetic education, he synthesizes the insights of educational theory and the humanities, for example, aesthetics, art history, and art criticism, in order to clarify for purposes of aesthetic education what the British philosopher Harold Osborne termed "percipience," which is essentially discerning and discriminating appreciation. Smith follows Osborne in equating percipience with appreciation and aesthetic experience. This is to say percipience is a power of mind that functions in our experience of artworks and other things from an aesthetic point of view. In this respect, Smith takes as the general aim of aesthetic education the preparation of well-informed art-world travelers and sojourners who have the capacity to perceive and understand artworks and aesthetic qualities "according to their own inherent intensities, their similarities and contrasts, and their peculiar groupings (Smith, 1989: 35–38). So far as the conditions of percipience are concerned, Smith discusses the requisites of synoptic vision, rapt attention, and consciousness of qualities and properties external to ourselves.

In addition to *The Sense of Art*, Smith's curricular recommendations are set out in the National Society for the Study of Education 91st yearbook, *The Arts, Education, and Aesthetic Knowing* (1992) in which, after mentioning a range of symbolic forms of human culture, including art, he says, borrowing a term from Artur Danto, that percipience constitutes the atmosphere in which we identify and experience works of art. The young gradually build a sense of art by moving through four phases of aesthetic learning: perceiving aesthetic qualities (K–3), developing perceptual finesse (4–6), developing a sense of art history (7–9), exemplar appreciative (10–11), and critical analysis (12). For Smith, teaching art involves preparation for "traversing the world of art with intelligence and sensitivity, which in turn presupposes capacities and inclinations I shall call 'percipience'" (Smith, 1992: 52). All that I add to Smith's analysis is the notion of "awareness" which is placed atop my aesthetic taxonomy (see appendix).

What Is Postmodernism Really?

I rarely use the term "postmodernism." I find that those who use it frequently are those who seem to know little about it, including its true origin. Postmodernism began as an international movement back in the late 1950s. At that time, it applied only to architecture as a reaction to the austerity of large corporate or public building styles. The most notable architect of the movement was Philip Johnson, who designed the Glass House in Connecticut, as well as the Seagram Building and parts of Lincoln Center in Manhattan.

The only reason I make an issue of this is that those who wish to be identified as postmodernists frequently seem to be more concerned about being heard or seen than about ensuring any values or positive qualities to develop as truly "hearable" or "seeable." This architectural movement has, in my opinion, a valid aesthetic agenda. I hesitate to say the same for much of the visual arts and literature (including poetry) parading under the umbrella of postmodernism.

Cultural Literacy and School Reform

We like to assume that we, as a nation, will continue to grow as a world leader in every way possible, including in the arts. It is true that the United States has more "quality" arts museums and galleries, far more major orchestras and playhouses, and at least as many dance companies, ballet and modern, as any other nation. Yet, most arts leaders whom I have questioned seem to feel uneasy about the general health of all the arts, with possibly the exception of the visual arts and architecture. Why? Most of us do not presume that we have the answers, but our questions are numerous and varied. Here are seven very basic questions:

1. Are the public and private school arts programs rigorous enough?
2. Are teacher training programs in the arts rigorous enough?
3. Have we emphasized some of the wrong things in arts education programs?
4. Has the assault on artistic standards created real problems, or are those problems just imagined by those who are often labeled "elitist" by detractors?
5. Can we achieve in the twenty-first century conditions in which artistic elitism and egalitarianism can coexist?
6. Can we achieve in the future conditions in which the arts will receive enrichment from our sociopolitical conditions and yet will not be driven by them?
7. What has happened to our popular music? Why is there no "golden age" as America experienced from around 1930 to 1960?

Some general statements addressing all seven questions are in order. Many teachers and administrators express awareness of a need for increased rigor in grades 8–12 arts programs, performing and nonperforming, but are apprehensive about the continuing lack of success in communicating such needs to parents and guardians of students. Over the past fifty years an intellectual battle has developed over the traditional arts vs. "open" arts. "The public is confused as to what art is. The word 'artist' probably appears in English-speaking nations as a malapropos more than any other in the vocabulary" (Olson, 1995: 161).

Populist movements or trends should enhance the arts; they have in Europe and Asia over the centuries to the extent that the arts use populist ideas and creations as sources, not as counterculture phenomena. Since World War II, the United States has experienced not only an increase in intellectual populism, but also a trend in entertainment that celebrates mediocrity and seems to reward the grotesque, the minimalist, the banal.

Early in 1994, the Goals 2000: Educate America Act, which established the National Education Standards, included the National Standards for K–12 Arts Education. As would be expected, teachers and administrators, as well as numerous politicians, hailed the legislation as much needed and a move in the right direction. Most important, in 1994 the National Education Commission on Time and Learning included the arts among the common core of learning in which all students should develop skills and understanding.

I believe that in most communities throughout our nation, rural and urban, most arts teachers, public and private, are very positive about these national standards; they believe that they can help overall in improving the quality of arts education in the schools. However, when the questions become more specific, many teachers find it difficult to give specific outlines and examples of quality improvement as well as examples of individual or collective success in their schools' arts programs. This applies to K–12 programs and post-secondary. Some occasional glimmers of hope shine through in the visual arts sector, but I suspect that much of that is through federal and corporate financed advocacy efforts, such as Getty Foundation activity and the Kennedy Center alliance and their beneficial spillover into various local art center programs, many of which have included impressive programs in dance: ballet, folk, and jazz.

SCHOOL REFORM AND THE ARTS

If the various states accomplish any school reform in the arts, it will most likely occur with the school reform networks in the forefront. Public schools have not been up to the task, not because of lack of qualified staff or budget, but rather because of politics. Several of the school reform groups have been in operation well over a decade, and continue to add schools, public and private, to their networks. Some of the longer running successful programs include the Accelerated Schools Project, Stanford University; the Coalition of Essential Schools, Brown University; Core Knowledge, Charlottesville, Virginia; Galef Institute, Los Angeles; and the Project 30 Alliance, University of Delaware.

In considering the first two questions, we might remind ourselves that, even with more than a decade of school reform, the issue of increased rigor in K–12 arts programs has not, in general, been taken very seriously. Relating to the third question, the same old observation holds true: the schools continue to allow the misconception that the arts are a frill, not an indispensable part of the program. Music and visual arts activities are scheduled, presented, and accounted for more as entertainment than as substantial academic areas.

The five school reform groups mentioned above work toward student mastery or achievement. For example, the Accelerated Schools serve "at-risk" students, and, in so doing, are constantly attempting to speed up and increase their learning by enrichment methods, which are usually employed in work with gifted and talented students (Levin, 1994). Avoidance of slow-paced learning and excessive repetition is central to the network's philosophy. Among its objectives are such approaches as inclusion of concepts, analysis, and problem solving.

The reform groups discussed herein would all be classified as comprehensive programs; they do not specify or emphasize the arts in the curriculum any more than they would any other subject area. Their comprehensiveness allows them to be valid models for inclusion of new approaches to learning in any subject area, including all the arts. All of the aforementioned groups have indicated that discipline-based arts, related arts, cultural literacy, and aesthetics will all have some place within curricular reform. The Coalition of Essential Schools (CES) maintains as one of its principles that each student will master a limited number of essential skills and areas of knowledge.

MODEL PROGRAMS

If, indeed, reform groups include arts study as an important component in their programs, some high quality model programs might be on the near horizon. They can not be aimless or disconnected series of exercises; they must allow for, and nurture, a sense of primacy in the arts in the search for the good life. Many of the groups to which we refer as model programs are often of this new reform network variety: public or private, supported by federal or private funds, or a combination thereof.

The Core Knowledge Program

Of the reform networks already discussed or cited, the Core Knowledge program is the one most closely connected with a developmental sequence. The program curriculum guide describes this sequence as "a consensus-based model of specific content guidelines that, as the basis of about 50% of a school's curriculum, can provide a solid, coherent foundation of learning for students in the elementary grades" (*Core Knowledge*, 1996: 1–4). The sequence presents a progression of specific knowledge in history, geography, math, science, language arts, and fine arts. At the beginning of each grade curriculum outline for the visual arts, a statement of purpose indicates its aim as helping children understand art as both doing and seeing: in particular, informed and active seeing—seeing as thinking and understanding "such that the concepts and works that the children study might begin to affect their own creative endeavors" (Core Sequence, 1–12). The visual arts guidelines include sometimes complex and technical concepts and terms that are germane to any study of the elements of art. Various artworks are included to illustrate concepts and terms. Most examples are relatively well known and can certainly be considered as items that should be in every educated

American's cultural and aesthetic vocabulary. In the *Curriculum Guide* the outline for music states that general goals of early grades music instruction are to help to develop an interest in and love of music. Similar goals are extended for the visual arts.

Edited by E. D. Hirsch, Jr., professor of English at the University of Virginia, the six-grade sequence formed by the *Core Knowledge* series makes an effective group of resources for elementary classrooms. Each of the six books in the series builds upon knowledge presented in previous books and is intended to be used as supplemental resources, not a substitute for the regular curriculum. In *What Your Sixth Grader Needs to Know*, the section on fine arts, comprising twenty-six pages of the total 382 pages, consists of two parts: music and visual arts. Poetry receives some modest attention under language arts. A challenging text for sixth grade, it is worthy of being included and cited as part of the school reform movement, with a very impressive section on the natural sciences. Music resources and tasks include ongoing instruction in basic music theory as well as some discussion of American music. The visual arts resources and tasks appear to be better thought out as challenging, yet truly informative, such as some nice approaches to understanding impressionism and abstraction in visual arts. We can probably find many things to criticize in the six-level *Core Knowledge* series, yet it is an effort that should be supported, as its reform philosophy and foundation is certainly a positive one.

The National Paideia Program

A well-rounded liberal arts education is the goal of the Paideia school network (headquartered at the University of North Carolina at Greensboro). Appreciation for and participation in the arts are becoming an integral part of the program, building the foundation for learning and cultural enrichment. The National Paideia staff believes that by allowing for different kinds of intelligences it can make available to students more opportunities for learning, and generally enhance the school environment. Part of the network's philosophy is to expose the students to a variety of experiences in which they can find opportunities to excel. The arts element relates to one of the Paideia Group's original principles: "Schooling at its best is preparation for becoming generally educated in the course of a whole lifetime, and schools should be judged on how well they provide such preparation." The most important of the three lifetime objectives of Paideia is the making of a good human life for oneself, but that is considered impossible without the fine arts being a component.

The fine arts program, which has a tendency to become specialized, should be, it is hoped, as fully integrated as possible with the work in the liberal arts. "Classical" education is founded in the notion that by attaining a certain degree of mastery in all subjects, continuing one's learning becomes a natural part of living one's life after formal schooling ends. Basic music theory, basic theories of design and color, an appreciation for the great masters of painting as well as for ballet, all serve as cultural foundations for integrating the arts into a framework of cultural literacy.

The Paideia program maintains the belief that a "classical" education which integrates the arts into the core subjects is not only possible, but is essential to the full development of a liberal arts foundation. The coordination of studying the arts with that of traditional subject matter is well suited to a varied approach which combines didactic, Socratic, and discovery learning. The didactic mode of arts instruction in areas such as color, design, light, music theory, history, musical forms, and performance combines with music seminars that are used as an introduction to a unit of study, a way of generating student interest in further investigation, and serves as an opportunity for individual artistic expression. A seminar upon completion of a class project can focus on not only what has been learned but also the learning process, itself. If such a completion seminar is indeed an established part of the program, there exists a built-in opportunity for the excursion into areas of critical thinking.

The seminar is a good opportunity for inquiry about any classical work of art. Exchange of great ideas, the object of any seminar discussion, provides the chance for an infusion of individual experience, adding personal meaning to a classical work that has engaged humanity through the ages. Students who view a slide of Westall's painting *The Sword of Damocles* (1812) for instance, might engage in a discussion of classical Greek mythology as relating to any of the following themes: power, responsibility, monarchy, wisdom, government, and judgment. This kind of approach allows teacher and students to bring meaning to artworks through associations and personal experiences. This becomes a very valuable learning-by-discovery approach, provided that the artwork, itself, remains the center of attention, and not merely a prop for social studies. In chapter six, Teaching Approaches, unit 13 presents the discovery of artistic style and meaning in another Greek classical moment, this time history rather than mythology, in Jacques-Louis David's painting, *The Death of Socrates* (1787). In this unit I have attempted to bring in historical and social context to enrich the learning situation. The painting, its form, textures, and colors, nevertheless, remains the real focus.

Arts in Basic Curriculum—South Carolina

The Arts in Basic Curriculum (ABC) program (headquartered at Winthrop University, Rock Hill, SC), like the other reform groups, is concerned foremost about the state of the school arts programs. The program emphasizes that the arts are indispensable. The goal of the program is to provide quality, comprehensive arts education.

The ABC program relies on the South Carolina Department of Education curriculum guidelines in dance, drama, visual arts, and music. Funded by the National Endowment for the Arts (NEA), the South Carolina Arts Commission, and the South Carolina Department of Education, the ABC program serves a broad spectrum, from magnet schools, to schools at-risk, to varied ethnic background neighborhoods. Members of the network agree that the at-risk school children receive a big boost. "The arts offer for disadvantaged children the one area [the arts] in which they are not disadvantaged. The arts can provide these children with ways of achieving success, giving them a feeling of pride. The arts are one area in which background is not a large determinant of success" (South Carolina Arts Commission, 1995).

Arts Partners

The New York City school system has developed a program that has recently increased the opportunities for students to participate in arts activities in a more open and exploratory manner. As a result, students can develop better and more enjoyable habits of studying and learning through inquiry methods that might enhance not only their arts experiences, but also other subject areas. Use of the terms "open" and "exploratory" often leave us with disappointment and misgivings. The unbridled rush for grants and other support leaves a trail of projects of very uneven and unpredictable quality. If the educational establishment can refrain from its power agendas and party lines, and truly follow a path of reform, dedicated to academic achievement and real learning skills, then critical thinking and awareness in the arts will finally become important partners in the curriculum, elementary school through graduate study.

Results from Reform

As a longtime university professor, over the years I had become aware of the continuing great need for more music listening experiences, particularly programs to give better opportunities to high school students for listening and learning about music of some aesthetic value and substance. As a result, with the assistance of music teachers from the public schools and colleges throughout Minnesota, and with some state grants, I formed the Minnesota High School Music Listening Contest in 1988 (see illustration 5.3). In 1991, Minnesota Public Radio signed on as a partner, and ever since, the program has continually expanded. The program currently is several times larger than in its nascent years.

Over the years, students have become well acquainted with a vast wealth of great music through this program, and many have realized some skills and insights not previously recognized. While there is no reference to reform in any information about the contest, I am certain that all of us involved in it

Ill. 5.3
1991–1992 Minnesota Music Listening Contest

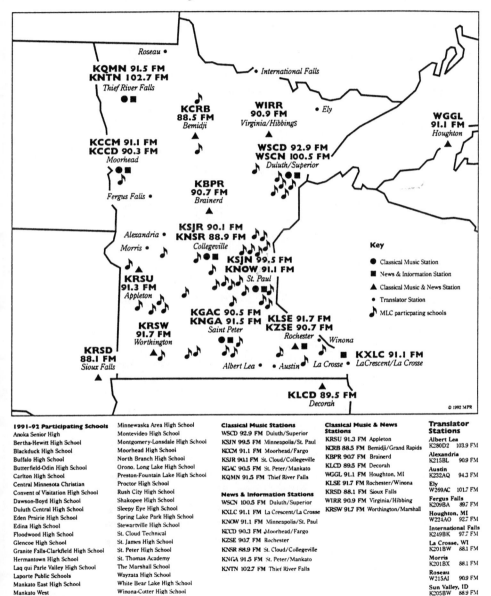

were probably feeling as if we were part of the mode of educational reform of the 1990s.

If the networks cited in this chapter develop programs to the point where member schools are able to realize objectives of student achievement and overall excellence, then the arts will have a friendly base for learning and exploration. As Paul Lehman, past president of the Music Educators' National Conference, has stated, "Education reform is currently a powerful force. We can take advantage of it to strengthen our programs. But we can do so only if we are willing to state clearly and precisely what it is that we want our students to know and be able to do. We must demonstrate that music (and the other arts) are subjects for sequential study and not merely an activity" (Lehman, 1994).

I believe that educators and parents will generally agree that the high school arts programs are currently at some kind of a crossroads. There are great differences among high school arts programs around the nation. Contrary to the same old rhetoric claiming that these differences are due to lack of federal or state funding, many of these differences relate very clearly to student motivation and attitude, parental attitudes, and what I like to think of as the neighborhood decorum, a "fitness" or "rightness." I also believe that most adolescents and young adults, with support from others beyond their peers, can develop skills in "receiving" ideas, concepts, facts, logic, and rational reasons for specific actions. Such skills have direct bearing on the individual's lifestyle, with influence spread across all human endeavors—the arts as well as science, literature, golf, to name a few.

To find meaning in the arts, high school curricula in the arts must include classes that devote time to the development of insights and skills for "receiving." This receiving skill requires individuals' ability to relate various artistic expressions and acts to their environment through experiencing/consuming. Other necessary skills would be using and developing the powers of analysis and imagination and the ability to interpret and evaluate both objectively and subjectively. Arts teachers for grades K–12 who find this paragraph a bit abstract for their liking should realize that such statements and objectives—perhaps with somewhat different wording and colorings—are commonly found in model courses of study as well as in some state curriculum guides. The reader will find in the thirteen units of chapter six, Teaching Approaches, that there are many dynamic and powerful things to be discovered and focused on among art works. Abstractions and metaphors such as line, color, texture, form, and unity become part of the mental adventure in the arts of which I have been discussing.

AESTHETIC MODELS

There probably will never be a time in the areas of education when we do not need models. Whether curriculum models or behavior models, they are often our initial line of action in improving, repairing, or establishing on-going programs that are successful. Idealized models are necessary. Good models, particularly in the arts, will include or be based upon universals that are amplified by specifics such as their historical, political, and social nuances. In order to find meaning in the arts, we usually engage in three modes: creating, presenting (sharing), and receiving.

When we are considering models for learning—or learning processes—in the arts, we cannot omit aesthetic process nor critical thinking. From an aesthetic position, we not only deal with the modes of creating, presenting, or receiving; we must add to all that the processes that tell us what, how, or why. That is, we deal with analysis and synthesis. When we do this, we engage in critical thinking. When we paint a landscape or a still life, when we compose a song or a flute and guitar duet, we are involved with all these things. This activity seems to be so strong in the aesthetic experience that it becomes part of its "character," and sets it apart from other cognitive and affective processes.

CULTURAL LITERACY

In recent years, the term "cultural literacy" has become somewhat confusing, mainly because of its misuse. When E. D. Hirsch spoke of this concept at the time he was bringing together ideas and approaches for the Core Curriculum, he was making reference to a core of learning that he considered necessary for any person to know in order to be a reasonably aware and intelligent person, able to communicate logically and with satisfaction. Several core programs exist around the United States that are not part of Dr. Hirsch's Core Knowledge network. The core concept, of course, is not new; it has existed for some time without enjoying much fanfare or any defining moments or developments. The core concept at the high school level, if it is to be of value in the arts areas, must realize several imperatives: (1) use of the inquiry learning techniques; (2) critical—and logical—links between elementary and secondary arts; (3) a cultural literacy that embraces a true multiculturalism; and (4) more study and writing "across the curriculum."

A Cultural-Behavioral Model

The position of the arts in our daily lives can be explained to some degree through a metaphorical cultural-behavioral model that takes into account both environmental and genetic factors. Such a model can comfortably represent (in abstraction) some of the relationships between critical thinking, cognitive style, and acculturation in relation to arts experiences. The model described here (Berry, 1976; Demick and Wapner, 1991) accommodates artistic phenomena well in that it attempts to comprehend systemic relationships among ecological, cultural, and behavioral variables, as well as genetic factors that partially include those qualities identified as talent or giftedness.

This paradigm is bi-level, with the upper half representing the more stable and traditional variables, and the lower half the variables that are the more changing and changeable. Observing the flow of the paradigm, we can determine that the background variables become subject to the process variables, ultimately producing the psychological outcomes. We can assume that Berry intentionally structured the paradigm in such a fashion that both upper and lower background variables are reciprocal, with the remainder of the model in a linear flow. This appears to be a dynamic, capable-of-change model, but with the capability of functioning as a cyclic continuum. Listed below are possible factors in such a schema (A and B represent background variables; A.1 and B.1 represent process variables; A.2 and B.2 represent process variables; A.3 and B.3 represent cognitive style):

Upper Background of the Model

A. Ecological Context (upper background variable) in an educational frame is determined by degrees of healthy home environment, history of good community schools, philanthropy, extracurricular arts activity, arts tradition, and value placed on learning.

We could devote a whole book to healthy home environment. In only a few sentences, however, we might best describe such a phenomenon as one in which there is always a pleasant situation of give-and-take, and one in which there is much inquiry and mastery learning. Communities have good schools only when the families are involved and aware of what the local schools can do, are doing, and plan to do. Those who want good music programs in their local schools must also fight for good science and math programs. If you doubt that premise, take a close look at individual schools in a school district; the chances are great that you will find the music, visual art, and dance programs to be better than average where the academics are especially strong.

A.1. Biological adaptation and ecological influence (upper process variables) will usually reflect parent input and initiative, community alliances, traditional connection between home and school, financial support to arts/performing groups, outside professional guidance, emphasis on future, long-term planning, value on "knowing" and "intellectual exercise."

Inclusion of philanthropy among the items of ecological context, is just as significant for public schools as it is for private schools and academies. In the larger urban areas such as New York, Chicago, and Los Angeles, public as well as private school programs benefit directly or indirectly from philanthropic giving. When we comprehend the large amounts of public funding supporting private school programs, as well as the private sources supporting public programs, we should realize that the ecological factor is more complex and important than we are usually led to believe. The last three items of ecological context are tied together. Extracurricular arts activity is truly an ecological factor, with the remaining two items, arts tradition and value placed on learning, being more philosophical. Psychological attending developments could almost be described as reciprocal cause and effect variables. All three are intertwined and interactive. It should interest school administrators that now and then one of the major news magazines will feature a particular school or program as a "shining light" from an area generally considered to be blighted, this because of the visibility of those three items. Their appearance can suddenly turn a besieged teacher, principal, or superintendent into a local hero with national coverage.

Parent input and initiative has remained over the years an indicator of a healthy school program—and specifically so with the arts. Individual parents, community groups, and parents' clubs are constant sources of support. An all-city art show or band festival, an appearance by a prominent dance troupe, actor, or poet often involve both intracommunity and intercommunity effort that is usually beyond the means and resources of any particular school district. All eight of the above items after parent initiative and input can be grouped together and all related to an important measurable factor: family participation in the educational enterprise, for which American education in the twentieth century has displayed a great need.

An important point should be noted here: for better or worse, the term "family" has come to mean more than the genetic relatives. Good examples of twentieth-century education have often involved the "community family" concept in a broad application. This has become a hallmark of modern American education, and nowhere is it more apparent than in arts programs. Raising money, outside professional guidance, and planning are so often part of the environmental family effort donated to the cause of aesthetic need and fulfillment, that we relate to good arts programs—elementary through post-secondary—as placing value on "knowing" and "intellectual exercise" through this community action.

A.2. Genetic transmission (upper variable) and cultural transmission (lower variable) in this model adapted to arts experiences will drive toward very different outcomes: the upper variable places more value on traditional arts and appreciation of arts as enduring aesthetic experiences, and the lower variable places more value on social commentary and "instant gratification" through the arts.

A.3. Cognitive style. In chapters two, three, and four, I have discussed in some detail both perceptual and cognitive processes as they relate to receiving, thinking, and communicating in the arts. I have consistently emphasized the position that in the arts the two processes actually overlap to various degrees. Gibson (1969), in her significant compendium on perception, speaks of "perceptual learning," giving special emphasis to such processes that are related to the arts in all modes.

I believe that it is essential for anyone involved in research, teaching, and curriculum development in the arts to have a basic understanding of the perceptual and cognitive style of their students. For example, with assurance from recent research, we know that field-independent students are usually more efficient in speed of information processing, allocation of attention, and visual search strategies. Thus, we can usually count on them for success in tasks that involve rehearsal, long-term memory, elaboration, and imagery.

We know that those who are field-dependent think more in a global fashion, and are not as attuned to the specifics as much as those who are field-independent. The field-dependent students will probably need more help in attending to relevant cues, subtle differentiations; yet they do rather well when dealing with whole structures, external form or structure of concepts, and focus on the critical features of the object. They profit by dealing with tasks by grouping what Thorndike (1984: 18) calls "chunking," merging words into larger units when those words are generating or applying to connected ideas. This helps in organizing short-term working memory. Thorndike has claimed that, as research demonstrates, to develop expertise in a certain field, one might develop the abilities to "perceive more complex aggregations of stimuli as unitary patterns" (Thorndike, 18). He believes that humans can enhance their powers of perception and memory of larger patterns of stimulus material.

Lower Background of the Model

B. Sociopolitical Context (lower background variable) is determined by the degrees of area schools academic/physical resources, problems/deficiencies, area employment stability, reliance on federal and state programs, reliance on political action groups.

For the sake of argument, we might ask why the first three items of the above list are included, that is, the schools' physical/academic resources, problems/deficiencies, and area employment stability. All three have been proven to have a strong correlation with educational progress without any direct reference to levels of spending. (As reciprocal factors, they each can be either cause or effect.) In fact, in William Bennett's report, data from the College Board and the U.S. Department of Education indicated that from 1960 to 1993 expenditures increased more than 200 percent, from 70 billion to approximately 250 billion dollars, and SAT scores declined 73 points (Bennett, 1994: 82).

The last two items in the group above are certainly related directly to spending. The great reliance on federal and state money for K–12 arts programs as well as higher education programs in the arts and humanities has continued to be a very contentious issue. In proportion to the vast amounts of money doled out by the two National Endowments (the Arts and the Humanities), only a smattering of evidence exists that can assure us that the National Endowment for the Arts allocations and awards are bringing about high quality results in the arts and arts education, and are the one sustaining resource for significant and deserving artistic projects which otherwise would not receive such backing. On top of all the contentiousness, we must keep in mind that the NEA is able to furnish only about 10 percent of the money received by arts groups for their sustenance. Private foundations and individual citizens are the main contributors. Our magazines, newspapers, and televised news have been telling us that we can no longer find many cogent relationships between our educational resources and measurable intellectual achievement throughout most of the United States. Barbara Lenner summarized it as follows:

What students actually learn seems small, debatable, or even nonexistent; here America provides the most poignant example. Though we rank first on measures of resources and resource allocation, we are currently not first on any measures of intellectual achievement. This appears to be true whether we compare American students with their counterparts in other developed nations, or with their predecessors in this country. (Quoted in Bennett, 92)

B.1. Cultural adaptation (lower process variables) will usually reflect a more surrogate influence from schools, churches, and agencies. McFee (1988) speaks of the problematic aspects of cross-cultural art. She considers questionable such thinking as "open" premises that all three modes of the arts—creating, presenting, and receiving—become totally contextual at every point, with "meaning" that becomes whatever you wish it to be. That, most assuredly, leaves logic, form, associations, and even memory to the mercy, or under the influence, of whatever cognitive and affective experiences the environment might be presenting at any given moment. The adaptation process is historically a key to progress of great civilizations. Excessive contextual and "open" approaches to the arts do very little to promote real cultural adaptation, however.

The lower process variables, the B-level, represent more the surrogate influences mentioned above. Those represented by the B-level are more reliant on schools, churches, community organizations, and government agencies. What social spending has been devoted to the arts shows itself not necessarily in successful arts projects, but rather in an increased need and expectation for grants and other assistance. This develops into an operational mode very much as has developed throughout education in the United States since 1960.

B.2. and B.3. Cognitive style behavioral framework of those individuals most influenced by the upper track (ecological-biological-genetic) will favor situations which are formed more on appreciation of traditions, yet, always in search of information, and would embrace the novel creation or the avant garde. They would probably be more field independent, not only conscious of details, but also how those details fit into the larger forms or worlds.

I also believe that those individuals most influenced by the lower track (sociopolitical-cultural-acculturation) will favor situations which move to embrace or deny national cultural modes. They might not be as information seeking, would be more populist, and would probably tend to be field-dependent, most aware and interested in the larger, less detailed, less defined issues and forms.

Defining Cultural Literacy (Again!)

It is unfortunate that in the United States we cannot approach the concept of culture without first ensuring that the discussants are in reality talking about the same thing. Until the 1950s the term "culture," as it relates to art, would mean by consensus: whatever had been learned by a group of people and maintained over generations, subject to modification and learned differently by some members of the society, wherein at its apex there can be a state of increased knowledge and refinement. This definition meets head-on with the anthropologists' approach to a definition in which there are belief systems of individuals in a given group or society. The anthropological cultural system rejects the dichotomy of literate and nonliterate, which is fine for a false kind of egalitarian approach. I am convinced, however, that this belief system, like the "open" philosophy (anything goes) is not compatible with the arts or arts education.

The Cultural Surrogates

Since 1960, the United States has undergone an alarming transition, one in which the public schools have attempted to serve as social surrogates in large urban school districts, in some cases preempting the instructional responsibilities of the institutions. As a result, three remarkable situations have developed: (1) urban schools have become entirely different institutions of learning when compared to rural and suburban schools; (2) funding for academic/classroom needs amounts to a smaller percentage of the total budget than before 1960, particularly texts, reference materials, library facilities and equipment, books, serials, professional library staff, and fully licensed, accredited teaching staff; (3) urban and suburban secondary schools have engaged in the "surrogate" style to the extent that there exists a strange mixture of arrogance and benevolence driving programs that emphasize the primacy of the "wisdom" of teachers, counselors, and administrators. Such wisdom usually pervades in terms of social policies and action, many non-academic items that should be left to the families of students, without any unwarranted type of indoctrination by school personnel.

The three situations mentioned above—there are many others—have much the same application to the arts as to any other parts of the curriculum (science, math, etc.). Consider this differentiation of urban and rural programs.

Data from the American Legislative Exchange Council for the 1992–93 school year reveals that the five states that year after year are at the top for SAT scores are well down in the bottom half for school expenditures (based on a formula allowing for differences in school populations). In 1993 the top-ranked states for SAT scores were Iowa, North Dakota, South Dakota, Utah, and Minnesota, in that order. The top ranked in expenditures—New Jersey, Alaska, Connecticut, New York, and District of Columbia (included for statistical verity of national data)—were all near the bottom of the SAT score rankings (Bennett, 82–83).

It is interesting that the five top SAT states cited are more rural than urban. If one does further searching, he or she will find that the quality of the rural programs is equal to that of many of the urban programs and far better than some.

Our Addiction to Federal Grants for the Arts

Everyone clamoring for more federal or state grants; increased competition and awards—it all begins to gather political dimensions. Advocacy groups evolve and politicians sometimes become involved. Review boards for both of the national endowments have developed into very doctrinaire groups. Anyone who has been involved in serious grant proposal writing since 1975 knows that proposals often had little chance if they were not loaded with multiculturalism of a kind and level that suited the social agendas of the review committees.

For those who are not financially secure, or are lacking in formal education, cultural adaptation, as it appears in the paradigm, could be interpreted as merely "going with the flow." However, it is more than that. Certainly, in the arts, it means more than merely surviving in a less familiar society than one has normally been accustomed to. It also means acculturation, that is, finding out information about a new society one has become involved in, and becoming well enough acquainted with the new society to participate in its activities—to be able to contribute as well as receive, and generally to feel at home.

Acculturation

The arts play a major role in acculturation. However, education in the United States has taken a strange turn in the last three decades. Large budgets have been devoted to the treating of hundreds of thousands of native-born Americans as if they were subject to this acculturation process. African Americans, Hispanic Americans, and Asian Americans have all been subject to this acculturation philosophy, when possibly the only group truly in need of such support are the Southeast Asian immigrants, who were not native born, and had little prior opportunity to learn the English language. It is ironic that so many immigrants from Southeast Asia have experienced relatively easy acculturation. As large numbers of the Hmong settled throughout the United States, these Asians have retained their "cultural memories" of their homelands, and have found it easy to share their culture.

Influence from Mexico

The Mexican style of the first half of the twentieth century—particularly painting and textiles—give us a remarkable reflection of the kind of cultural-behavioral model discussed earlier in this chapter. Mexican visual and temporal art gives evidence of systemic relationships among both elitist and populist, as well as among genetic and environmental factors.

During the first half of the twentieth century, with the world-wide spotlight on modern expressionist abstract painting, one might think there was little other than nonrepresentational visual art, particularly with the prominence of cubism. From 1900 to 1950, particularly during the period of 1920 to 1940, Mexican music, dance, fiber arts, pottery, and mural painting exerted great influence upon the aesthetic outlook in the United States. Mexico led advances in modern art, including decorator art and "public" art. By the time of the New York World's Fair of 1939–40, Mexican and Brazilian art, music, and dance had captivated America, both North and South. In the heart of Manhattan one could encounter Mexican music and art at the top floors of such skyscrapers as the RCA Building and the Empire State Building. It was all around us; it influenced Americans much more than the general public realizes, or even than Mexican Americans themselves realize.

Of all the creative effort influencing America, the two great muralists Diego Rivera and Jose Orozco were the most important. While studying in Spain and France, Rivera was influenced by the work of Cézanne. When he returned to Mexico, he promptly began numerous murals for schools, hotels, and public buildings. His murals contained some socialist propaganda. Orozco also involved his painting and mural work with social reform themes. Both artists received a warm reception from the general public as well as the critics in the United States. As Sheldon Cheney (1963) stated, Rivera and Orozco "have, without weakening of the abstract structure, restored art that is socially meaningful, even instructive and thought-provoking. They have widened the boundaries of modern painting" (Cheney, 637).

The Social Agenda and the Arts

Whatever propagandizing there was associated with the art of the two great Mexican painters, there was always an "aesthetic command," plainly some kind of artistic value easily recognized. After 1950, however, Latin America, like the United States, began to sag under the burden of social reporting and propagandizing. You can hardly expect to see an exhibit by art students and faculty of major U.S. universities which does not have a sizable portion of the displayed works devoted to social ideas to the point of nonart phenomena. This should not surprise us. It has happened before and will continue to happen. The great Russian composer, Dimitri Shostakovich, with all his brilliance, could not overcome this same "functional purpose" burden imposed on him by his government from time to time. His poorest efforts were those which had socialist propaganda objectives. An example of such effort was his massive cantata for massed choruses and orchestra, *Song of the Forests*, which praised the USSR reforestation program.

In this chapter we have continued to focus on the arts as they are shaped and experienced through critical thinking processes. We might find that areas and topics, such as the mind, aesthetic analysis, and everyday life drives us toward more singular ground in which everyday experiences within the world of arts should probably present its most puzzling and contentious facets. However, these are not in the areas of creativity, presentation, or performance, but rather in the modes of receiving such as observing, listening, and analyzing. The areas of receiving are where we seem to be lacking. No matter whether or not we refer to curriculum, instructional method, or administration, improvement in these areas is not dependent upon money or long-term endowments as much as it is in need of attentive minds. Educational leaders and their institutions have overlooked or played down these all important "receptive attitudes." Various degrees of interaction with a work of art will range from casual to very intense. A stroll through an art gallery will not ensure aesthetic experiences, nor will combining listening to a symphony orchestra on radio while doing household chores (Knobler, 13).

Even writers such as sociologist Allan Bloom have contributed much to the discussion of American education and its failures, and have included the arts in their discussions. It is easy for us to be responsive to Bloom's position in his *The Closing of the American Mind* (1987) that our high school and college populations in recent years have included a large proportion of students who have become indifferent to traditional studies and approaches to learning (Bloom, 34–41). He strongly suggests that young people of the United States have become less learned and less motivated to study languages and literature.

Unfortunately, Bloom's references to the various arts become sketchy. Only music receives specific attention, and those references sadly confuse art and entertainment as if there existed little difference between them. I mention this, not to be hypercritical of a fine work, but rather to use it as evidence of a general lack of conception by the public of the dual track of music as art and music as entertainment, along with the many fascinating gradations in between. This dual track, as described earlier in this text, is understood by the small percentage of those individuals involved as arts creators, presenters, or serious receivers, yet is not well known by the 90 percent or so of the rest of our nation.

As we anticipate chapter six, Teaching Approaches, it would seem to be helpful to consider some of the thirteen units in terms of their objectives and how those objectives relate to the topics of concern, such as perceptual style, cognition, conservation, images, and aesthetic analysis. In unit 1, which is visual, emphasis is on aesthetic analysis of "public art." Social context becomes important. In unit 2, which is music, a primary objective of the work is to explain and bring to life this concept of conservation. By detailing the concept with a theme and variations example, we rely on models. Unit 4, which is a cubist painting, focuses on novelty, newness, divergence or convergence, all important factors in creativity and aesthetic experiences. Units 6 and 7, both music, become exciting opportunities to work with mental templates that often involve the concepts of divergence and conservation. The final exercise of the group, unit 13, considers an eighteenth-century painting, *The Death of Socrates*, by the classical master, Jacques-Louis David. This is a fitting unit for closure for the group, as it gives us an opportunity to consider numerous factors within the focus-and-discovery format, factors defined and considered throughout chapters two through five, such as: characteristics of the art object, the creator, social context, perceptual aspects, brightness, colors, images, management of form and perspective, atmosphere, contrast, historical context, and idealization.

6

Teaching Approaches

The following units are all based upon a method of focus and discovery. The emphasis is upon viewing and listening with an "internal goal," such as becoming familiar with a work that is not only well known, but that also has qualities which make it interesting and worthy of study. It has things "to study about." These can all be classified as adventures of the mind.

UNIT 1. PAINTING

Jose Clemente Orozco, *Zapatistas*

Focus: Orozco and Diego Rivera were Mexico's leading painters of the twentieth century. Both were known for their large murals which frequently depicted social issues. A sense of rhythm is very evident in *Zapatistas*.

Discovery: A part of Emil Zapata's army of peasants pass in review. The rhythm is the most exciting element in the work. The repeated lines of the men on foot and those on horseback emphasize that rhythm. The strong feeling of marching is obtained by overlapping planes that tilt forward, as if a bit downhill. Contrast of light and shade adds to the dramatic effect.

Additional Study Suggestions: Find examples of murals by Rivera. Do murals of this kind all have some social message or theme? Are there presently any living artists in the United States who are known for painting public murals?

UNIT 2. MUSIC

"Camptown Races" (Dave Brubeck: *Dave Brubeck's Greatest Hits* [Columbia CS 9284])

Focus: An old Stephen Foster melody used in a sophisticated theme and variations form laced with free improvisation. As an example of "third-stream jazz," it presents us with many opportunities to identify and enjoy musical details and ideas that have both "classical" and "popular" characteristics.

Discovery:

a) Listen for the theme and variation approach in the composition. Find it in other compositions:

 1. *Variations on "I Got Rhythm"* (George Gershwin [Angel S–36070])

 2. "Button Up Your Overcoat" (Peter Nero: *Peter Nero in Person* [RCA LSP–2710])

 3. "Trout" Quintet, Andantino (Franz Schubert [London 41019])

b) Discuss the concept of variation. Listen to, and discuss, the processes of variation of a theme, the developing of a motive, and the extending of a theme or motive as found in:

 1. Haydn, Quartet in C Major, "The Emperor" (2nd movement)

 2. Beethoven, Symphony No. 5 (1st movement)

c) Compare the variation concept with improvisation:

 1. Differences

 2. Similarities

 3. Identify examples of improvisation in jazz

 4. How about organ music? Did J. S. Bach improvise?

UNIT 3. MUSIC

"Badinerie" (Swingle Singers: *Going Baroque* [Philips PHS 600–126])

Focus: A "hot" jazz vocal rendition of a well-known section from the Bach Suite No. 2 in B Minor, it keeps the original masterpiece intact. The seven singers making up the group at the time of this recording have note-worthy backgrounds. All are French and classical musicians. Two are classical singers, three are both professional singers and accomplished pianists, one is a prize-winning pianist, and one is a violinist. The director, Ward Swingle, is the only non-French member. He was born in Alabama, and studied music in Cincinnati, Ohio.

Discovery: Before listening to the Swingle Singers version, become ac-quainted with the original composition, for flute and orchestra, from the Bach suite. Notice that the badinerie is a lively, playful dance in duple time. It was popular in the seventeenth century and was a frequently used form in the Baroque era suite that were often composed as concert pieces during the eighteenth century. The suite—it could be either for orchestra or keyboard solo—was a favorite form of Bach.

Additional Suggestions:

1. How were the voices used in the Swingle version? As instruments?

2. The singers' use of da—ba—da syllables.

3. Except for the jazz beat by the bass and drums, was the Swingle version similar to the original?

UNIT 4. PAINTING

Pablo Picasso, *Les Demoiselles d'Avignon*

Focus: This is considered by many to be the first cubist painting. To some viewers, the work is at first a bit shocking. The figures of the women seem forced into angular and rough forms.

Discovery: How did Picasso exhibit cubist characteristics or qualities in this painting? Separating forms into geometric units and then "unnaturally" reassembling them. Treating objects as multi-sided shapes and figures which make you feel like you are never seeing all there is to see.

Additional Suggestions: Compare Picasso's cubist paintings to those of his contemporary, Georges Braque. What are the similarities and differences? Why do we connect Picasso so closely with Igor Stravinsky, the composer? Some thoughts? They were contemporaries. The art works of both sometimes shocked. Both were "experimental"; they sought the novel, the never-done-before. Both had a solid understanding and respect for the art forms of earlier periods.

UNIT 5. MUSIC

Sky, Feast, and The Circular Word (Richard Stoltzman, clarinet: *New York Counterpoint* [RCA 5944–4–RC])

Focus: These compositions offer a stimulating group of New Age music, a hybrid space jazz. Richard Stoltzman is well known as a clarinet virtuoso. He has performed with many of the world's great symphony orchestras, and has recorded frequently with them.

Discovery: Listen for the atmospheric combinations of both electric and acoustic instruments. Exotic sounds are achieved by the use of "foreign" instruments. Can you identify these instruments in the three pieces, respectively?

"Sky"—Riqq, an Egyptian instrument

"Feast"—Pandero, a Spanish drum

"The Circular Word"—Ramana and Thon, Thai drums

Notice that all three compositions have a wide tone color spectrum, using the following instruments in background and partnership with the lead clarinet part:

• piano	• shakers
• electric piano	• string bass
• synthesizer	• bass clarinet and bassoon
• triangle	• various percussion (including the exotic ones)

Would the term "jazz improvisation" be applicable to the clarinet part in the three compositions? How does this jazz compare with that of John Lewis and Dave Brubeck? What are differences or similarities in their improvisation?

UNIT 6. MUSIC

Bach on Wood (Brian Slawson [CBS M 39704])

Focus: Music of Bach, Corelli, Handel, Pachelbel, and Vivaldi is performed on electric bass marimba, concert grand marimba, acoustic and electric vibraphones, orchestra bells, xylophone, and gold and silver chimes, as well as a full array of entuned percussion instruments ranging from timpani to tam tams and two-octave cowbells. Just about every possible untuned percussion instrument found in ensembles is included with even a few curiosity items such as alarm clocks and a cross-cut saw.

Discovery:

Listen to the traditional performance of the following:

Vivaldi, *The Four Seasons*, "Winter"

Bach, "Jesu, Joy of Man's Desiring"

Bach, Concerto in D Minor for Harpsichord and Orchestra, Allegro

Corelli, Concerto Grosso, Op. 6, No. 8

Pachelbel, Canon in D Major

Compare the Slawson arrangements with the original works as performed in their traditional instrumentation. Has the arranger been careful not to distort or change the music of the original score?

Compare *Bach on Wood* with other similar approaches:

Going Baroque (Swingle Singers [Philips PHS 600–126])

The Unusual Classical Synthesizer (Westminster 8182)

Switched-On Bach (Carlos [CBS MS–7194])

Rameau (Bob James [CBS MK–39540])

Bachbusters (Don Dorsey [Telarac DG–10123])

All of these examples vary greatly in their timbre (color), but are similar in their intent to be faithful to the music itself: the melody, harmony, and rhythm as intended by the composer. Only the tempo seems to be changed from time to time.

UNIT 7. MUSIC

"My Melancholy Baby" (Phil Mattson and the P. M. Singers: *Jubilee* [Doctor Jazz FW 40527])

Focus: This is a sensational example of jazz singing.

Discovery: After listening to "My Melancholy Baby," find earlier examples of jazz singing. Consider the following discussion and study topics:

1. Vocal groups of the Swing Era, e.g., the Modernaires

2. Groups of the Fifties, e.g., The Four Freshmen and the Pied Pipers

3. Solo Jazz singing's "golden age" (1930–1945): June Christy, Rosemary Clooney, Anita O'Day, Nat "King" Cole, Ella Fitzgerald, Bessie Smith, Helen Forrest, Lilian Terry, Mel Torme, Billy Eckstine, Billie Holiday, Big Joe Turner, Ma Rainey, and Sarah Vaughan

4. Present day jazz singers: Etta Jones, Morgana King, Cleo Laine, Chris Norris, Joe Williams

5. Present day jazz vocal groups: Jazz Crusaders, L. A. Jazz Choir

Try to determine the differences between the various jazz vocal styles: blues, scat, bop and vocalese.

UNIT 8. MUSIC

The Bridge Game (based on J. S. Bach's *Well-Tempered Clavier, Book I*) (John Lewis and the Modern Jazz Quartet [Philips 826 698–1])

Focus: John Lewis, born in 1920 in Illinois, lived much of his early life in New Mexico. He began piano study at age seven. After serving in the army during World War II, Lewis studied at the Manhattan School of Music in New York City, and began playing and arranging for Dizzy Gillespie, Charlie Parker, and Miles Davis. About 1950, Lewis formed the Modern Jazz Quartet with Milt Jackson on vibraphone, Ray Brown on bass and Kenny Clarke on drums—all formerly with the Dizzy Gillespie band. The modern Jazz Quartet has recorded more than forty albums, and is internationally recognized as one of the best models of modern third-stream jazz performance.

Lewis' formal musical training in New York City allowed him to handle all musical styles—traditional, European-influenced, and jazz-influenced. Most important, it allowed him to work with the combinations of jazz and the traditions of the concert hall. He composed string quartets, ballets, works for large orchestra, and film music, as well as his modern third-stream jazz.

Lewis has often stated that two of the most important and sustained musical influences on him have been Bach and Duke Ellington. He found the music of Bach to be a most inspiring source of ideas for his improvisations. It is because of this that the music cited here retains much of its eighteenth-century contrapuntal style.

Discovery: Notice that these several Bach Prelude and Fugue settings use different instrumentation with a variety of choice of violin, viola, guitar, and bass added to the piano part at various times.

UNIT 9. MUSIC

"Yesterday" and "Hey Jude" (Francois Glorieux: *Francois Glorieux Plays the Beatles* [Vanguard S 31–6410])

Focus: Two of the most popular and enduring melodies by Beatles Lennon and McCartney are brilliantly arranged and performed by Francois Glorieux.

a) "Yesterday" in the style of Chopin
b) "Hey Jude" in the style of Bach

Discovery: After listening to the two Glorieux arrangements, study various Bach and Chopin keyboard works.

a) Is there a characteristic Chopin style?
b) A Bach style?
c) In this extended form are these Beatles tunes any longer just pop tunes?
d) Is this "serious" music, or could it be made over into larger forms, the same as has been done with folk tunes over the centuries?

UNIT 10. MUSIC

Wolfgang Amadeus Mozart, Piano Sonata in C Major, K. 545 (1st mov.)

Focus: Like his piano concertos, Mozart's piano sonatas set the standard for those that followed. All of Mozart's piano sonatas were in three movements, always in a sequence of fast—slow—fast.

Discovery: The first movement, allegro, is in sonata design (similar to the first movement of many symphonies). Listen for the classic sonata design in the first movement (a three-part design).

EXPOSITION	DEVELOPMENT	RECAPITULATION
Main theme		Main theme
Episode (bridge)	Main theme broken up; Key changes and melodic variations	Episode
Theme 2		Theme 2
Closing group		Closing group

Further study: Listen to this same movement by Mozart performed in a "New Age" version by the hot jazz, classical, and fusion group, Free Flight, which is entitled, *"Mo's Art"* (Free Flight: *Slice of Life* [CBS Records #FMT 44515]). Discover the similarities between the original and the contemporary arrangement. In this brilliant modern work, which far transcends the usual pop styles of today, can you discern the conservation principle discussed in chapters two and three?

UNIT 11. MUSIC

Variations on "I Got Rhythm" (George Gershwin [Angel S–36070])

Focus: This represents the stylized jazz form developed into a larger art form: the use of a popular tune as the theme for a series of variation treatments.

Discovery:

a) Introduction based on opening motive of song; theme stated by piano

b) Variation 1: wandering piano; theme in brass and percussion (Note transitions between variations)

c) Variation 2: slow with violin sobs

d) Variation 3: fast, Chinese; piano with full orchestra

e) Variation 4: jazzy, then bluesy, with arpeggio ending

f) Variation 5: fast, still jazzy, plus a Hollywood style building to end

Further Study: In 1932, after a visit to Cuba, Gershwin wrote his *Cuban Overture*, which he based upon the rumba and habanera rhythms. Like the *Variations*, the *Overture* presents melodies that are extended. The rumba and tango rhythms dominate the *Overture* and are themselves extended and varied. This dancelike overture was a timely one; the rumba and tango were the most popular of ballroom dances during the 1930s and 1940s, even overshadowing the various versions of the "jitterbug."

UNIT 12. MUSIC

Improvisation on Theme of 'Rokudan' (**Ravi Shankar [Deutschegrammaphon #DG415621–4]**)

Focus: As the guitar has acquired increasing importance in our American Music today, it can be compared with another fretted instrument, the sitar, which has been in the center of music in India for some time.

Like jazz performers, the Indian musicians follow a pattern in which they create spontaneous musical ideas or improvise on existing melodies. By following such structural patterns, the musicians are able to play together by interrelating melody, rhythm, pitch level, and tempo into a unity.

Ravi Shankar, considered to be one of the greatest of India's musicians, is certainly the best known throughout the world. Shankar plays the virtuoso instrument the sitar, a plucked instrument with six tone strings, and 19 sympathetic strings. Because of the complexity of Indian music, many tuning adjustments are needed.

Discovery: This composition brings together traditional music of the East with the forms and style of Western culture. It is an interesting combination of Japanese melody and Indian form and method. There is a thorough development and extension of seemingly European influence. Most of the recorded music by Shankar seems to rely heavily on extension and development of melodies and rhythm patterns.

UNIT 13. PAINTING

Jacques-Louis David, *The Death of Socrates*

Focus: David, one of the great early classical period painters, is remembered mainly for his portrayals of ancient Greece and Rome. He drew inspiration and imagination from classical antiquity for some of the most structurally articulate works in the history of art. As a friend of the French Revolution, David painted with a desire to inspire a love of democracy among other ideals. Critics appraising this popular work of the late eighteenth century, describe it as having a sparseness and solidity, with brilliant management of forms, perspective, and atmosphere, so that even with all the vibrant hues, and the strong contrasts, the artist was able to focus the interest on the central figure, Socrates.

Discovery: As an example of idealistic art, *The Death of Socrates* probably was intended to purvey a message: Socrates as the model for ideals, for rational and moral conduct, someone willing to die in defense of those ideals. Most viewers of the painting would agree that David's remarkable talent and insight give to us idealized, nearly perfect human bodies in elements of great pathos as well as sculpted forms often too perfect to be real.

Further Study: Consider the previous statement above. Is it possible to bring together very many characteristics of idealized art in describing this work?

Appendix

A Taxonomy for the Aesthetic Transaction

Does the field of Aesthetics need a taxonomy? The answer might depend on the background of the individual being addressed. I remind the reader that the term "taxonomy" traditionally refers to a science or scientific technique for classification, such as we find in the fields of botany, zoology, and agronomy. Benjamin Bloom and colleagues (1954 and 1964) presented their benchmark project in an attempt to provide for classification of the goals of our educational systems. Both the cognitive and affective taxonomies have become well ensconced in the study of education, particularly in any reference to learning and teaching processes within teacher training programs.

This aesthetic taxonomy has much the same characteristics as those already described. However, it does not relate directly to objectives; it relates purely and pointedly toward identification, naming, and classification of processes and phenomena. I think of this not as the "final word," but rather as a "dynamic start" which could serve as a model, and possibly stimulate further research and study in the area of experimental aesthetics. It represents a dynamic *schema*, as it is generative and allows for possible change or expansion.

The taxonomy consists of four stages: associative, abstractional, conservational, and absorptive. The stages move in a hierarchical fashion, with three columns representing the initial perception processes advancing or evolving to the state of awareness, the left column representing the sequence of accentuation, the right column representing cognitive attention, and the middle column interactive between the other two in a process that moves from initial perceptual and conceptual actions and becomes the heart of the taxonomy's *schema*. The third and fourth stages, conservational and absorptive, lead to more metacognitive conditions.

A GLOSSARY OF TERMS FOR THE AESTHETIC TAXONOMY

The terms found in this short glossary are in two categories: (1) those which might not be familiar to many of the readers, and (2) those that are generally familiar, yet are grounded in different context and meaning as they apply to the literature and study of aesthetics and information theory.

abstracting process—expressing qualities or characteristics apart from a particular person or object, drawing ideas from objects or phenomena that are not, in reality, part of them.

accentuation—a process that combines both cognitive and affective potential.

acculturation—the process of adopting the cultural traits or social patterns of another group.

activation—a memory process of association in which one cognitive activity triggers another cognitive activity.

aesthetic paradigm—any model or plan that describes some kind of interaction between subject and art object involving any or all of the three aesthetic modes, creating, presenting, and receiving.

affective—that which pertains to emotion or feeling, also intuitive actions in contrast with cognitive.

asymptotic—of functions that relate to infinite series of phenomena, becoming increasingly exact.

cognition—the process of knowing, perceiving [note: cognition and perception appear in tandem in any aesthetic *schema* with perception as the primal sensate process].

critical dimension—pertaining to the status, value, or quantity at which characteristics of a system of logic undergoes change.

critical thinking—a disciplined process of analyzing, synthesizing, or evaluating information resulting from observation, reasoning, or reflection.

developmental sequence—a hierarchical process extremely necessary in aesthetics and critical thinking processes.

entropy—measure of sameness, a uniformity which brings about a lack of distinction or differentiation.

intention—a general concept obtained by abstracting from various objects as "first intention" or abstraction of ideas and images of sensate objects and "second intention" or abstraction obtained by reflecting on "first intentions."

metacognitive—of "higher order" thinking, critical and reflective.

stasis—a state of equilibrium caused by opposing equal forces.

stochastic—a randomness in a series of observations.

syncretism—interaction between imagination and flexible reasoning, a key ingredient in creative processes.

In Figure A.1 *A Matrix for the Taxonomy for the Aesthetic Transaction*, the entire schema is outlined. Although the matrix represents the four levels, from associative, up through abstractional and conservational, to absorptive, the three upward vertical columns represent the specific processes involved.

Fig. A.1
A Matrix for the Taxonomy for the Aesthetic Transaction

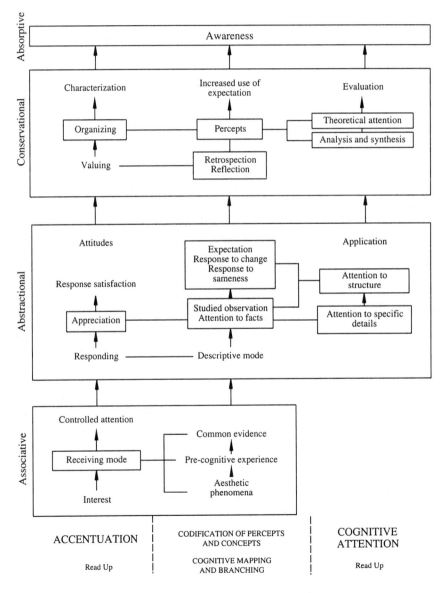

STAGE I: ASSOCIATIVE

I.1. Interest

1.1. *Random attention.* Sensitivity to a musical task or event at its most rudimentary stage remains in a random state. An example can be drawn from a situation such as a cocktail party in which there are possibly dozens of simultaneous conversations accompanied by recorded music and a large variety of physical movements. Sensitivity to the music, in its randomness, would probably be limited to a very incomplete processing of neural information. Psychologists refer to certain examples of this as uncontrolled attention or nonselective attention. Thus, the music would be subject to five different kinds of processing: (1) excitatory responses, (2) inhibitory responses, (3) on responses, (4) off responses, and (5) on–off responses (Lindsay and Norman, 1977).

I.2. Receiving Mode

2.1. *Image retrieval.* Two processes become apparent at this point, association (or associative learning) and what might be called, "activation." Activation of appropriate memory structures will serve to control the cognitive system. "Activation comes at a price. You cannot simply set off the subconscious mechanisms to do things without paying for it" (Lindsay and Norman, 1977: 592). The price is simply a lower effectiveness at the more powerful conscious mechanisms. Retrieve one detail and others will often enter. "Whenever the subconscious processes get going actively, they will use up some of the limited mental resources available for normal daily activities. Thus, the ability to carry out even simple activities, especially planning and decision making, is curtailed" (Lindsay and Norman). This presents no problem, however, as we recognize this in certain levels of musical activities, and have even coined phrases such as "head in the clouds," "in a fog," and "in another world." One activation theory (Broadbent, 1958) cites studies demonstrating human response to auditory level as they relate to pattern development. Broadbent (125–27) summarizes activation theory in a manner that may be described in the following equation-like diagram:

amount of awareness of:

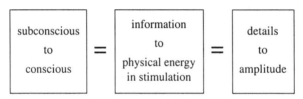

As the conscious is activated, information (fresh patterns) is proportional to the sensate stimuli (visual and auditory stimuli involved in retrieval of the patterns).

In turn, the information level determines the level of awareness of musical details, in the same way as the amount of sensate stimuli determines the amplitude.

The subject of amplitude has many intriguing perceptual applications here. Amplitude of form (extension of space), amplitude of emotion, light, decibel level, or Hz (cycles per second) level, all have a part in activation, as they all help to bring the patterns into focus. Maximum information relating to novelty and complexity is influenced by some aspect of amplitude. Some individuals' musical experiences do not go much beyond this rudimentary level of receiving; their pattern associations remain in a "comfortable" redundant state. Their experiences are more of the banal than the adventuresome.

In music and visual arts, activation and associative learning are in tandem. As the attention is focused on the stimuli, that attention is determined by the information load or amplitude, enhancing the conditions for "learning," which will at the next high levels of aesthetic transaction call upon short-term and long-term memory (see Suppes and Ginsberg, 1962).

I.3 Aesthetic Phenomena

3.1. *Environmental factors.* Registrations (mental impressions) are indeed influenced by one's psychobiological—perhaps the term sociophysiological, is preferable—surroundings and background. Miller and Colwell (1982) include in a list of registrations such factors as historical, cultural, and personal associations. These factors provide the footings for stage one of the aesthetic transaction and, in time, often determine the scope and intensity of the aesthetic experience.

3.2. *Internalization.* Size and complexity of patterns perceived as units increase with development of skills. In precognitive experiences the subject begins to bring together phenomena and facts or feeling and perception as a continuous process of internalizing.

3.3. *Relating social context.* The environmental conditions are considered here as not only social conditions but also conditions brought about by physical limitations or opportunities.

I.4. Precognitive Experience

4.1. *Preperceptual storage.* An auditory persistence begins to appear in the form of a sensory or "immediate" memory that retains stimuli prior to analysis. It is, in effect, an acoustical storage of tones and noise bursts. Preperceptual storage systems function so that the perceptual systems need not be directed to the stimulus at the time of presentation, allowing for im-proved recall because of increased time for perception (Underwood, 1976).

4.2. *Externalization.* Whether it be listening, composing, or performing, musical activities take on forms of individual or group expression that will undergo continuous redefinition: "Musical experience may enter the labor of individuation and thus become as intimate as is the coming to terms with life and death. I believe that the universal power of music has its roots in this direct immediacy" (Fraser, 1985). As our sensate impressions mix with expectations and memories, we are often moved to externalize, to express in ways that lead to new forms or abstractions.

4.3 *Specific ideas in short-term memory.* The more opportunity an indi-vidual has to engage at some level of any of the three modes of aesthetic activity, the richer his or her accumulation of specific ideas will become. This will become a stepping point between short-term and long-term accumula-tion of concepts and images.

I. 5. Common Evidence

5.1. *Integrative processing.* As memory becomes a more important fac-tor at the higher levels of the taxonomy, there is a very important interaction between sensory and contextual information. The immediate sensory memory becomes what Underwood (1976) calls the precategorical acoustic store (PAS). As sensory information is processed out of the PAS, it interacts with con-textual information relevant to the stimuli and retained from previous stimuli. This interaction is illustrated in Figure A.2., the design taken from a model of language interaction by Underwood (1976: 28).

5.2. *Sensory effects.* Changes in the sense organs and along the sensory pathways occur as signals are carried to the central nervous system. Such changes increase sensitivity. As our auditory organs increase our sensitivity to musical sounds, they also help to increase our ability to perceive detail in those sounds. Berlyne (1971: 65) reminds us that "there are indications that sensory channels may be blocked or relatively desensitized at times of un-usually high arousal, suggesting that the aroused organism becomes more selective than usual, concentrating on stimuli that are of prime importance while diminishing the distracting effects of others." This would suggest that the more intensely we focus our attention on specific musical sounds or col-ors, forms, textures, the more our sensory effects are in tandem with central effects. Figure A.2. displays and emphasizes a very clear progression from sensory information toward pattern recognition.

This same general process occurs continuously through the aesthetic transaction, most prominent in the third stage (see stage III. 4.4.).

5.3. *Attention and memory.* Regular features of our musical environment, such as tonal patterns, rhythms, and forms, which we recognize as "fitting" into our world, do not need to be focused upon in order for us to operate in

Fig. A.2
Integrative Processing of Musical Information

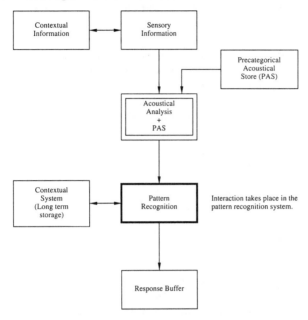

This same general process occurs continuously through the aesthetic transaction, most prominent in the third stage (see III. 4.4).

our musical environment. Whenever unexpected or deviant musical events appear, attention is evoked and the input is processed at a high level of consciousness. We have the ability to selectively process those parts of the painting or music stimuli we see or hear that are of interest to us, focusing upon them so that they are vividly perceived. Other ideas (stimuli) are not rejected in the process, but they do not have the perceptual synthesis that those attended have. When attending to one musical or visual segment, the observer reconstructs it internally, thereby allowing it to be assimilated into his active auditory or visual memory. Unattended musical ideas may attract some notice only when they are noteworthy to the observer, or play an important part in the overall scheme; they have contextual probability (Underwood, 224). Otherwise they are stored only in preperceptual memory which will last for a relatively short time. "The purpose of the attention process is to admit to consciousness only one perceptual hypothesis at any one time" (Underwood, 208).

I.6. Controlled Attention

6.1. *Pattern recognition.* As we attend to musical or visual stimuli, our selectivity at the end of this first stage allows us to begin a rudimentary phase of conceptual thinking. Concepts will be abstracted from empirical knowledge. For example, melodic contour as well as figures, forms, light, and shade can be remembered independently even though the object consists of figures, trees, or buildings; and pitches or interval sizes, as the concept of contour as line and direction is abstracted from it. This appears to be supported in recent research. In music, "the contours of brief, novel atonal melodies can be retained and retrieved from short-term memory even when the sequence of exact intervals cannot" (Dowling, 1978: 346).

6.2. *Satisfaction associations.* The truism that learning is enhanced when the subject's attention is focused on the stimuli to be learned—attending to an artistic idea or event—leads us to the importance of associations at this level. Associations are contiguous, that is, they are formed by a chain of the central representations of events (Wilson, 1980: 241). Examples of such associations might include the twentieth-century composer Igor Stravinsky writing a composition, "Pulcinella" (ballet and suite), in eighteenth-century style, associating one form of information coding with another as a result of recoding. Two or more entities thus are linked in association (Wilson, 105).

When attention is focused on associations that are incorporated into networks and series in which there are multiple lines of activation, not only is learning enhanced; the "satisfaction potential" is enhanced.

Hypothesis. The satisfaction potential reflects the processes which lead into stage two of the aesthetic transaction. The satisfaction potential will serve an activator for the "responding" phase, and all ensuing phases. It will remain as the most important single factor in the paradigm. As an accentuation factor, it combines both cognitive and affective potential.

STAGE II. ABSTRACTIONAL

II.1. Responding

1.1. *Highlighting.* Selective response or filtering in artistic events seems to bring about a kind of highlighting as represented in Figure A. 3.

Seldom are we involved in musical experiences where there is not always, at a given moment, some melodic line, interval, chord, rhythm pattern, or coloring that has salience. This highlighting is essential to stage two. The Gibson "Developmental Sequence," a model of perceptual phases, was inspired by Piagetian concepts of development stages. It places great emphasis on the abstracting process as does the entire stage two of this taxonomy. The Gibson model functions as a cybernetic pattern.

1.2. *Centration.* The term, "centration" was employed in Jean Piaget's studies to denote a tendency to fix attention on a dominant feature or some significant characteristic of it. In music, centration might occur as inordinately powerful highlighting at the expense of nonhighlighted features. Some music researchers (Pflederer, 1967) regard centration as negative, a cause of inaccuracy and incompleteness. In painting, it can contribute greatly to dra-

Fig. A.3
Application of Gibson's Developmental Sequence

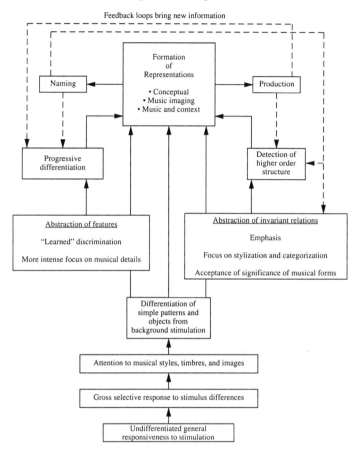

matic effects, for example, lighting directly on a face or object in a painting by Rembrandt. This taxonomy recognizes centration as having the potential for both a negative and a positive power of information transmission.

1.3. *Syncretism.* In all arts experiences a subject who does not keep apart the phenomena and facts or the feeling and perception is one who "syncretizes." Syncretism is a process of interaction that involves imagination and creativity as well as flexible reasoning (Gibson, 1965).

II.2. Appreciation

2.1. *Context.* Relating musical experiences as cognitive or affective events to our world around us is a natural process. Excessive contextualism, that is, story association, religious, moral, political, ethical emphasis or bias reduce rather than enhance the artistic quality. Great compositions of sacred or nationalistic nature are as such because they are works of art in which the artist has expressed his feelings and ideas; they are not contrived for a specific nonart purpose, such as political campaign songs, protest songs, political murals, or vignettes.

2.2. *Abstraction of ideas*. Subject-object interaction will determine the attitude of attention. Such an aesthetic attitude can be defined as "disinterested and sympathetic attention to and contemplation of any object of awareness for its own sake" (Stolnitz, 34). "Disinterested" refers to attention that is given not for ulterior or functional purposes, but simply for the musical experience itself. Abstraction of ideas from the music during this mode of disinterestedness contributes to an attitude that will allow for unfettered aesthetic experience leading to understanding and appreciation, free from contextual excesses.

II.3. Descriptive Mode

In contrast to the previous phase, this phase is bound to contextual events. Semantic memory develops. As semantic information is processed, inferences are made. Such inferences can be of empirical, propositional, or speculative nature. They will have a strong relationship with imagery later in this paradigm.

II.4. Studied Observation (Attention to Facts)

This portion of Stage 2 will constantly recur throughout much of the paradigm. This is certainly a "guidepost" factor in the aesthetic experience. It becomes essential in determining the nature and degree of our receptiveness.

4.1. *Maintenance rehearsal and short-term memory*. For many subjects, music presented forms a mental trace, just as visual arts do. Often both auditory and visual memory are needed. However, in music the observational trace decays rapidly, but can be restored by rehearsal (Broadbent, 1958). This process of rehearsal is an introspective repeat or review of an item that helps to "maintain" it in the short-term memory store.

4.2. *Audiation*. Audiation (Gordon, 1985) is much the same as maintenance or rehearsal, applied specifically to music. It not only involves the short-term maintaining, but also an integrative long-term memory store. "Audiation is the hearing of music in one's mind when the sound is not physically present. One may audiate in recalling music or in composing music. In contrast, aural perception takes place when one hears music when the sound is physically present" (Gordon, 34).

Hypotheses. At this point the taxonomy must, by nature, reflect a transition from sensate and affective dominance to cognitive dominance.

II.5. Attention to Specific Details

5.1. *Integrated rehearsal and multiple processing.* Every time we hear the same composition, it will be different from previous hearings. Our minds form categories so that we can respond to the similarities between musical events rather than the differences. Such processes lead to the development of prototypes. These prototypes might be considered as musical "gestalts," whole compositions or sections that are entities in themselves, and are often identified by such terms as "schema" or "frame" (Purcell, 1984). In our musical experiences, we are constantly matching percepts of current frames with prototypes stored in our memories.

While the visual images in painting and sculpture seem easy and natural enough to understand and accommodate, the "inner images" connected with music are no less real, even though their existence is rather difficult to verify, as they are things of the mind. Thus, as we consider mental images associated with experiences in music, dance, sculpture, and painting, it becomes necessary to argue *ad rem* for the recognition of inner visual images in the creative, productive, and receptive modes for all of the arts.

5.2. *Selective attention.* Similar to the processes at the beginning of stage two, selective response and attending result in a form of highlighting. We begin to select out, to filter certain properties. When satiated or bored with particular series of events, we then engage in diversive exploration seeking new or different events such as sounds and colors (Berlyne, 1971).

II.6. Response Satisfaction

6.1. *Reinforcement and associative experiences.* Our brains appear to have in their neural networks some kind of stimulus amplifiers which facilitate feedback. These amplifiers are identifiable with centers of the midbrain that have been found to exert reinforcement effects upon direct electrical stimulus. This becomes a rather critical point, not only in this paradigm, but in any consideration of music or visual arts response, associations, reinforcement, and satisfaction. As these brain mechanisms are activated, the neural changes involved give a reward stimulation. The process is intuitive. Reward stimulation affects choicemaking and reinforcement, causing selective learning and memory.

6.2. *Emotional generation.* Works of art present to us environmental stimuli which contain unexpected or novel values. The effect upon us "constitutes a blocking of an ongoing response which results in attention and further activity and emotional experience. The extent of the response and the type will govern the characteristics of the emotion experienced" (Purcell, 192).

"With a few exceptions, all stimuli that are registered by the nervous system have motivational effects, including the physiological indices of emotional impact" (Berlyne, 1971: 113). Except for those that evoke unlearned reflex reactions, various stimuli evoke an orientation reaction, a name given to a psychobiological process of only seconds' duration at the point of initial sensory stimulation, resulting in increased arousal.

II.7. Attitudes

Expectancies govern behavior. That behavior can be divided into two aesthetic attitudes: generalization and discrimination. The rational tendency to generalize is basic to forming attitudes. It involves "intention," the process of abstracting ideas or images from sensate objects or events (Kellogg, 1985). The rational tendency to discriminate is motivated by two things, environmental sensitivity—that is, a sensitivity to presented patterns or forms—and preferences based upon that sensitivity.

II.8. Expectation

8.1. *Response to change.* Two responses are basic: acceptance of innovation, and recognition of either of the conditions of stasis or disequilibrium.

8.2. *Response to sameness.* Recognition of stasis or disequilibrium is, in like manner, basic here. The condition of entropy must be considered at this point. As a process state that is experienced intuitively, entropy represents a condition in which there is the maximum amount of information (Shannon, 1949). Maximum musical information, or originality, is carried by messages in which all the sonic units have equal, or nearly equal, probabilities of occurring. Consider atonal music: a twelve-tone row contains maximum information. Compare such a pattern with a pop or folk melody that relies on frequent and repetitive use of relatively few tones, thus containing less information. The redundancy of the folk or pop melody is more obvious. However, in music, redundancy is not necessarily a problem as opposed to speech communication theory, wherein it is "a measure of the relative 'wastage' of symbols in transmitting a given message" (Moles, 42). Entropy in musical application could represent lack of order or form due to stasis and the condition of sameness. To achieve balance we must also have variety.

Musical events have meaning for us when they cause us to expect other musical events (Meyer, 1956). Expectation is built upon memory which influences our sense of probability through sensitivity to forms, styles, and harmonic practice.

II.9. Attention to Structure

9.1. *Data-driven processing.* In music, data-driven events lead to conceptually driven events that are retrieved from memory. In considering attention to structure, many similarities between music, dance, painting, and sculpture should be emphasized at this point.

9.2. *Recognition of familiar structures.* On the importance of structure: "The response to complexity of form and perceptual organization I would argue is a fundamental aspect of the way we organize our experience of the world. Stimuli which are both complex and perceptually well-organized are intrinsically interesting and attractive" (Purcell, 209).

As we attend to various aspects of the art object, and begin to categorize patterns, we are involved in what Sloboda described as "global" analysis (Sloboda, 1978: 323), which precedes any detailed analysis in perceptual processing. A global view of a specific melodic line would focus on the approximate positions of the musical tones and contour, visual shapes, lighting, and colors thus formed. This processing will continue and appear in a more advanced level at stage three.

Listener, performer, and composer must all be concerned with "basic shapes" or gestalt patterns, as they are constantly encountering unified groupings of tones, phrases, themes, sections, and movements that have a "cumulative" identity. We think—or we are capable of thinking—of Mozart's *Haffner* Symphony or Tchaikovsky's *March Slav* as whole compositions if we are familiar with them. To some theorists, the Grundgestalt, or basic shape can be a tonal or harmonic application, wherein a function of a musical idea in a tonal work is to contribute to a coherent tonality of the whole.

II.10. Application

In the aesthetic transaction, the subject's receptors have a maximum limit to the flow of information. When the subject's limit of information flow is exceeded, he makes choices (preferences) of forms from the material presented to him, based upon previous experience. "Forms are abstractions, elementary stages of intelligibility. If these criteria fail him, the individual is overwhelmed, left behind by the originality of the message; he loses interest" (Moles, 74).

Hypotheses. Aesthetic transaction cannot be sustained without some redundancy and *a priori* form and meaning.

STAGE III: CONSERVATIONAL

III.1. Valuing

The process of valuing is both conscious and subconscious. As we "determine" values we integrate information such as overall impression, dimensional comparisons, and focus on the object, as well as our own degree of arbitrariness, discretion, and creativity.

III.2. Retrospection and Reflection

Within the process of valuing we have experienced two phases: attitude development and theoretical reflection and retrospection. The second phase exists because of the need for us to justify our likes and dislikes. Reflection and retrospection are among the very highest order of human capabilities; they often result in, or contribute to, the development of aesthetic models or exemplars.

III.3. Organizing

3.1. *Sensory information storage.* Abstracting and filtering emerge here as processes which are essential for the next level, development of percepts. Abstraction is a process for discovering critical dimension. It occurs when an invariant relation is discovered over a number of varying objects or events (Gibson, 1969: 108). Musical or visual events that present contrasts, or are embedded in different contexts offer relationships which can be literally extracted in conscious or subconscious search. At this point we can find differences between visual arts and music. The added difficulty of a temporal nature in the storage and organization of sensory information in music makes it more of a challenge. In reference to musical events, this abstraction is a form of "dissociation" as compared to "association."

This dissociation becomes an important factor in recognizing certain musical examples as being "stylized." The "Birch Tree Carol" is a simple— it might be called bland—Russian folk song in its original form. However, it has become stylized in several compositions of larger dimension, notably in the finale of Tchaikovsky's Symphony No. 4. "Camptown Races" is a simple folk-like song by Stephen Foster. In the complex jazz setting by the Dave Brubeck Quartet, however, it has become highly stylized. While there have been elements of association that could stimulate conservation, such as the invariant of basic melody, the transformations are so great that the discriminations center around how the various treatments of the invariant differ, for example, rhythmic transformations or melodic alterations. The irrelevant random material is filtered out; "rival" stimuli is filtered out.

3.2. *Recall and recognition.* As memory structures are used, they remain more accessible for future use. When the mind attempts to retrieve some poetry detail from memory, it will almost always bring back additional details, even if they are not wanted. As examples, consider the following model: While rehearsing or listening to "How Lovely is Thy Dwelling Place" by Brahms, a conductor finds himself thinking of the composition "How Lovely are the Messengers" by Mendelssohn, because he had used it recently with his church choir. The Mendelssohn composition is part of background processing that consists of automatic, well-learned structures. As data-driven processing, it has distracted him, limiting his mental resources available for planning, analyzing, or other activities directed toward the Brahms work. Subconscious operations mold old knowledge into new combinations, but conscious activity is necessary to evaluate what has been molded.

III.4. Percepts

4.1. *Categorical perception.* If the function of perceptual learning is to mediate the perception of objects in the environment, then arts perception refers to the extraction of information from the specific environment through experience and practice. Such experience and practice, in itself, generates stimulation.

All perception relies on the brain's exact registration of all qualities and variations in sensory patterns that are subjected to the combining and integrating of "certain of these qualities resulting in a new construction—a percept which is not isolated, but exists as a part of a systematic categorization of experience in concepts and schemata" (Vernon, 1954: 14).

4.2. *Grouping.* Categorical perception results in cues, transformations, and a "fusion" of dimensions of difference, all leading to enhancement of cognitive experience. Transformations include such things as changes from a smooth to a disjunct melodic line, changes in meter, retrograde, and changes in size of performing body. Recognition of various changes are possible through grouping or "chunking." Thorndike (1984, 18) gives evidence that "expertise in a given field may involve in part the development of the ability to perceive more complex aggregations of stimuli as unitary patterns" (18).

4.3. *Encoding.* Cues in the musical stimuli, mostly of a semantic nature, consist of definitions and criteria. Bruner (1957: 123) states that these cues are important in "inferring the categorical identity of a perceived object" (123). Encoding becomes a system of building categories to which various stimulus input can be matched. Sets of cues might be grouped under the three dichotomous headings: (1) relevant or irrelevant, (2) conditional or adaptive, and (3) reward or rejection. Conditional cues contribute their whole effect toward correct responses (Restle, 1955: 11–19).

Long (1965) found that compositions by composers such as Milhaud, Hindemith, Shostakovich, and Prokofiev did not offer "discriminating power among young or inexperienced subjects," as it might to the musically sophisticated (151). Discrimination becomes a learned concomitant of encoding.

4.4. *Concepts.* Aesthetic responses are "the result of a difference between the characteristics of a particular environment and the way it is organized and remembered and the existing cognitive structures concerned with ongoing everyday experience" (Purcell, 189–210). Concepts of generalization and differentiation emanate from such responses. These concepts can guide and direct, as well as be guided and directed by, perception.

a. Audiation. At the stage two level, audiation occurred as a mental trace. Here at level three it appears as a more sophisticated group of events. Hearing music in one's mind without the sound of it actually being present, has a strong connection with both internal visual images and internal auditory images. There might be any number of image states, each state embracing a different position of the template, which is an internal prototype image. As the template becomes larger and clearer, and has more specificity, the relative power of the visual and auditory images is affected, as is the power of the audiation.

b. Mnemonic states. Certain memory builders help us to conceptualize. The process of template forming is one; and when we are able to use templates for matching, we are involved in a high order of differentiation.

c. Conceptualizing vertical and horizontal patterns. Sensitivity to concepts of macroforms relies on such ideas as linear gesture, sections, resolution, decay, and closure. Some theorists maintain that even in atonal compositions such as those by Anton Webern and Arnold Schoenberg, there is often some kind of linear gesture that brings to them a tonal order and restraint which contributes to artistic coherence and direction (Lewis, 1981: 84–97).

4.5. *Recognition of invariants.* Abstraction, a process for discovering critical dimension, occurs when an invariant relation is discovered over a number of varying objects or events (Gibson, 1969: 108). Musical events that present contrasts, or are embedded in different contexts offer relationships that can be literally extracted in conscious or subconscious search. In reference to musical events, this abstraction is a form of "dissociation" as compared to "association."

Centration and decentration are internalized responses relating to the presence or absence of invariants. "Centration is a kind of compulsory fixing of attention upon some aspect of a stimulus display; it is thought to result frequently in distortion of perception" (Gibson, 1969: 343). It is possible that the individual who is musically mature and sophisticated, captures stimuli with his aural and visual behavior. The musically inexperienced or less sophisticated is captured by the stimulus. Therefore, the musically inexperienced is probably more subject to global aspects, more attracted initially to the most obvious.

Those who are field independent appear to be less likely to be involved in centration in their musical experiences. They are able to perform tasks of musical conservation, that is, they can retain an image of, and sensitivity for invariant musical ideas that appear in various transformations. For example: in the "Trout" Quintet, Op. 114, Franz Schubert included an andante movement that was a theme and variations built on the melody of "Die Forelle," one of Schubert's better known lieder. The "trout" melody is the invariant; it undergoes five transformations (variations, in this case), yet remains recognizable by those who perceive the various similarities in each transformation.

III.5. Theoretical Attention

5.1. *Analysis and syntheses.* Musical improvisation offers some interesting observations. The performer who is improvising, be it organist or jazz performer, and the perceptive listener share a kind of creativity. Both must rely on categorical information as prototypes, the performer in order to perform logically, the listener in order to understand fully.

Ongoing experience, therefore, consists of matching current perceptual input to stored prototypes. Where a sufficient mismatch occurs, as when unexpected objects [sound] are present, we pay attention to and engage in extra processing of information about that aspect of the external situation (Purcell, 192).

Therefore, both are involved in an analytical phase of aesthetic perception; and, equally important, they are both involved in a synthetic phase as well. According to Berlyne (1971: 135), the synthetic phase allows subjects to recode continuously information into "supersigns," patterns of many signs or symbols.

5.2. *Markov states*. Modern information theory presents to us new models of cognitive mapping and branching that help greatly to explain the mental processes relating to higher orders of perception. A. A. Markov (d. 1922), a Russian mathematician, developed stochastic (processes governed by the laws of probability) models that offer analogies for probabilities of changing states in information processing. In the Markov process, future values of a random variable are statistically determined by present events and dependent only on the event immediately preceding. A Markov chain is a process involving discrete random events; it is stochastic in nature.

Any model of associate learning represents branching that can be related to information chains or sequences. Such a model would be particularly appropriate in music and dance as temporal art processes, and possibly drama. Any branch (continuous route) is a sequence of joint events necessary to reach a particular state on a particular trial by a particular route. The learner samples a population of elements of a stimulus situation from trial to trial. This sampling reaches a critical stage as it becomes asymptotic.

Asymptotic applications can be given to musical response. Within the aesthetic transaction (with no distinction between listening and performing), an infinite series of semiconvergent functions (some actually divergent) develop so that the sum of the first few elements give an increasingly strong approximation to a specific function that continues on to approach a given limit, or continues to infinity. For example, in a music class a teacher might guide the students in finding similarities between symphonies of eighteenth-century composers and those of nineteenth-century composers. The convergent elements might include such factors as number of movements, instrumentation, treatment of main and subordinate themes. The divergent elements would be highlighted by marked differences in the musical "color" at various moments. This would all progress toward a condition which one might relate to critical thinking and metacognition. If this paradigm is viable, then the students might be on their way to finding an aesthetic perspective in which they are able to hear and visualize such things as the eighteenth-century emphasis on the rational, the orderliness, and balance in comparison to the nineteenth-century emphasis on color, exoticism, and subjective feelings. The students might develop such insights that by the completion of the course, they find pleasure in developing in their minds such perspectives as eighteenth-century classicism and nineteenth-century romanticism. As asymptotic processes, teachers and students discover that, along with the differences, similarities exist. The romanticists retained the classic penchant for form, and they developed their harmonic structure and rules much in the style of the classicists. These discovered similarities and differences continue on and on, each listening or performance experience different, one from the other.

The asymptotic state might be considered essential in the processes of musical response and reinforcement. Response occurs as a result of learning, but it also occurs in the learning process, itself. Reinforcement in the musical experience, listening or performing, takes place through such two-state response, and is either or both sequential or random. The transaction would now involve three variables: magnitude, intensity, and duration.

To illustrate, let us consider the elements of music. As a composition progresses, the listener/performer experiences it as some kind of organization in an ongoing temporal setting. The rhythm and melody move in an event-to-event fashion, always closely related and interdependent, yet never completely convergent. After several bars of music, we obtain an increase in expectation for what we feel we might continue to hear. Sometimes our expectation is realized, and some times the composition "fools" us because the composer has presented to us patterns that we did not retrieve from our short-term or long-term memory. Hence, we obtained "fresh" information. The more such information we store in our memories, the more complex, adaptable, and sophisticated our expectation responses become. Like the composer, the listener and performer are also constructing (and reconstructing). Current experimental research seems to indicate that "musical training is associated with the adoption of an analytic and sequential processing mode toward melodic information, and suggest that long-term training in complex cognitive skills has functional neural concomitant" (Davidson & Schwartz, 1977: 58).

5.3. *Neural concomitants.* Patterned neural activities associated with information processing in the brain are imaged in electroencephalograph tracings as event-related potentials (ERPs). Recorded from noninvasive electrodes attached to different areas of the scalp—frontal, parietal, and central—these ERPs contain a series of components characterized by positive or negative peaks. Early components of 100–200 milliseconds (ms), based upon a one-second (1,000 ms) brainwave, or potential, exist mainly as physical stimulus parameters. Some of the later components (300–700 ms) only exist in conjunction with cognitive and perceptual processes. One of them is the P3 (positive 300 ms) complex.

The entire P3 complex is believed to reflect mainly the encoding tasks of preprocessing, feature extraction, and identification. This offers positive ground for the consideration of the P3 complex as a reflection of such musical and visual arts events as generally involve analysis and synthesis, and specifically involve pattern recognition, interpretation, discrimination, and intention (the abstraction of ideas or images from sensate events).

Some of the earliest application of waveform analysis to musical response that goes beyond the alpha wave identification, is the identification of the P300 series effect difference between persons with "absolute" pitch and those without it. Klein, et al. (1983) obtained results that support the theory that the P300 is an indication of the updating of working memory. In a presentation of visual stimuli, letters H or S, for sixty milliseconds on a screen, and auditory stimuli of 1000 and 1100 Hz sinusoidal tones for sixty milliseconds, the control subjects (non-absolute pitch) showed standard ERPs in both visual and auditory modalities. The absolute pitch subjects showed standard ERPs in the visual modality, but showed a smaller ERP (P300) elicited by the auditory stimuli.

The researchers correlated the P300 amplitude of each of the subjects with the percent of correctly identified tones for each subject in the Absolute Pitch Test. The higher the test score, the smaller the P300. Several accounts of the absolute pitch phenomenon suggest that "subjects with this skill have access to permanently resident representations of the tones, so that they do not need, as the rest of us do, to fetch and compare representations for novel stimuli. Our data are consistent with the interpretation that the P300 is a manifestation of such comparisons" (Klein, et al., 1308).

Hypotheses. With a study by Kutas and Hillyard (1980) as a model, the following hypothesis and design is given: To determine if EEG tracings will reveal ERPs resulting from musical incongruities presented to twelve human subjects. They will listen to three sets (pairs) of musical examples. In each set, the first example will be correct. In the first set, the second example will have a moderately incongruous note injected; in the second set, the second example will have an obvious and strongly incongruous note injected; and in the third set, the second example will have one note that is tonally correct but augmented. It is hypothesized that notes occurring out of context will be associated with specific types of event-related brain potentials (ERPs). Each moderately and strongly incongruous note will elicit a series of negative potentials, whereas each note that is correct tonally, but augmented, will elicit a late positive series of potentials.

The development and enhancement of systems designed to present an accurate representation of a specific human's response to a specific musical event could have many far-reaching applications, notably: (1) opportunities for experimental studies of the aesthetic transaction which no longer rely solely on speculative and descriptive information, but on detailed psychobiological data as well; (2) new directions in music pedagogy enhanced by closer scrutiny of the individual's reactions to different kinds of musical events, and to various levels of satisfaction and success; and (3) opportunities for a new look at some of the more serious curriculum problems in music education today; access to real data on stimulus–response processes in musical experiences.

5.4. *Memory: short-term and long-term.* Our musical memory, like memory in general, functions as a primary system dealing with specifics, and as a secondary system dealing with more general aspects. This bilevel concept of specific–general activity does not sufficiently explain musical memory processes. For a more suitable explanation, we must relate more to short-term memory or long-term memory, and to the retrieval of musical information presented in sequence of order and structure. Serialization and sequence become a higher order problem of syntax (Lashley, 1951).

Perceptions arise when sensations are integrated and supplemented with information other than the most current stimuli. That information is retrieved from short-term or long-term memory. Audiation remains significant in the process as it offers maintenance rehearsal in short-term memory, and integrated rehearsal when retrieving long-term memory. Maintenance rehearsal keeps the material "fresh" in the short-term store. Integrative rehearsal draws out the material from the long-term store. Therefore, the perception is conditioned (learned). (See Hebb, 1949.)

Hypothesis. The integration is bimodal: visual and auditory.

III.6. Increased Use of Expectation

For many centuries the music of Western civilization and much of Eastern music has developed around some kind of tonal stability. Even atonal music of this century will often have a linear system that merely replaces the "traditional" one. Lewis (1981) speaks of this linear system as it relates to a composition by Alban Berg, concluding that, "To assume that because a piece exhibits a strong atonal structure it may not also depend upon tonal direction for some part of its coherence runs the risk of doing an injustice both to the flexibility of musical art and to the subtlety of the minds that create it" (Lewis, 84–97). The coherence that is a product of the system remains a determinant of the degree of musical expectation at any moment. As a stochastic process, expectation will depend on what we have already heard.

The invariants in musical conservation support the process of expectation. However, at this higher level of the aesthetic paradigm, two other processes appear to merge and become inseparable from conservation: interpretation and imagery. Interpretation, or decoding, allows us to set up a system of opposites: affective versus cognitive, connotative versus denotative, and semantic differentials versus concrete imaging. All three pairs of opposites give impetus to the process of expectation. As we interpret, we form images and conserve at the same moment. The great accuracy and detailed visual memory make eidetic imagery an invaluable concomitant of conservation. We store visual patterns as well as auditory patterns. Composers of program music are involved with eidetic imagery in various degrees, and those listeners who know of the program are also involved with eidetic patterns, transcendental though they might be. Indeed, eidetic imagery is one of the ultimate results of expectation. Some of our richest aesthetic experiences come from the understanding of and sensitivity to programmatic music as well as to music in which interest and appreciation is generated by meaningful forms, gestures, and coherence.

III.7. Characterization

"Characterization" in this taxonomy implies the process of categorizing, but with a wider spectrum of perception and memory retrieval, being involved in both creative and analytical processes. There is inductive activity at the level of perception.

In perceiving two discrete but similar baroque concertos, one might find shapes and intensities that correspond: they fit into a single category (e.g., fast–slow–fast). The perceptual system processes the data of the patterns and considers a small number of high probabilities (likely rules), which can then continue to test a wider spectrum of related rules, which, in turn, might involve, directly or indirectly, many others (Leeuwenberg, 1971: 307).

III.8. Evaluation

As the final level of the third stage, evaluation represents those processes that bring together all the conservational aspects of this stage. It is at this point that the musical invariants are assessed and stored, or retrieved.

Abstract percepts have now allowed for the development of abstract concepts that represent intelligence playing over a natural scene. At this point in the paradigm, values are intrinsic; music is valued for itself. It is treated now as something that evokes ideas or feelings. These ideas and feelings are sources of enjoyment or displeasure.

STAGE IV. ABSORPTIVE

IV.1. Awareness

1.1. *Accentuation.* Accentuation relates to a unifying quality that brings together objective and emotional perception. For all perception some degree of emotion is requisite, even if it is no more than a little bit of excitement generated by the attention that brings the object into focus (Olson, 1984).

Order—Disorder

Predictable—Unpredictable

Banal—Original

Redundant—Informative

Intelligible—Novel

Simple—Complex

Finally, accentuation evolves from phenomenal experiences that combine with noumenal experiences that are based upon purely reflective, speculative, and intuitive thought.

1.2. *Association and mental images.* Art stimuli, generally imperfect or inconsistent, specify properties of the object, not the object, itself. Therefore, stimuli often have only limited validity as indicators of objects; they are cues (Brunswik, 1956). Our powers of music and visual arts recognition and recall begin to function most aptly as a process of mediation begins. As our minds extract information from stimuli, they mediate the messages, attending more and more to distinctive features and invariants. This all contributes to higher order structures whereby there develops a perceptual pick-up of structural regularity, redundancy, symmetry, novelty, balance, variety, and repetition.

The process of "intention" involves the abstracting of ideas or images from sensate objects or events. Intention might be viewed as a higher order process that is related more to experiences of art, rather than mere entertainment.

Eidetic imagery is a long-term application of intention, yet the accuracy and detail involved move it far beyond the limits of sensate events. Aesthetic experience can involve eidetic imagery related to a totally abstract or "absolute" musical or visual form, or even a specific musical score.

Introspection in aesthetic tasks contributes to awareness through "vigilance" tasks (Saldanha, 1957). Such tasks are yet related to long-term memory and eidetic imagery, even as they increase blocking and filtering of images and ideas.

1.3. *Details.* At this final level there is a vital concern for progression, regression, and probability. These are inherent in the hierarchy outlined throughout this paradigm. Information probability (see III.5.1.) existed earlier on in asymptotic states, and now at the highest level it exists more in an ergodic state in which over varying periods of time there occur:

1. compounding of stimuli.

2. sequential reinforcement of ideas or events.

3. reticulation (networking) of ideas or images.

4. absorption of semantic cues.

5. implanted value judgments from long-term memory.

6. images of continuity and relatedness.

Attention to details reaches its ultimate state, the highest order of aesthetic awareness, in this paradigm: a selflessness resulting from "sympathetic attention to and contemplation of any object of awareness for its own sake" (Stolnitz, 1960: 35).

Selected Bibliography

Alho, K. *Mechanisms of Selective Listening Reflected by Event-Related Brain Potentials in Humans.* Helsinki: Academia Scientiarum Fennica, 1987.

Allport, F. H. *Theories of Perception and the Concept of Structure.* New York: John Wiley & Sons, 1955.

Apel, W. *Harvard Dictionary of Music.* Cambridge, Mass.: Harvard University, 1956.

Arduini, A. *Principles of Eidetics: Outline of a Theory.* New York: Springer–Verlag, 1992.

Arnheim, R. "Gestalt Theory of Expression." *Psychological Review* 56 (1949): 156–71.

Attneave, F. *Applications of Information Theory to Psychology.* New York: Holt, Rinehart & Winston, 1959.

Attneave, F., and Olson, R. K. "Pitch as a Medium: A New Approach to Psychophysical Scaling." *American Journal of Psychology* 84 (1971): 147–66.

Bartlett, J. C. "Cognition of Complex Events: Visual Scenes and Music." In *Cognitive Processes in the Perception of Art.* Ed. W. R. Crozier and A. J. Chapman. Amsterdam: North-Holland Publishing Co., 1984. 225–45.

Bartlett, J. C., and Dowling, W. J. "Recognition of Transposed Melodies: A Key Distance Effect in Developmental Perspective." *Journal of Experimental Psychology* 6 (1980): 501–15.

Beardsley, M. C. *The Aesthetic Point of View.* Ithaca: Cornell University Press, 1982.

Bender, J. W., and Blocker, H. G., eds. *Contemporary Philosophy of Art.* Englewood Cliffs, N.J.: Prentice-Hall, 1993.

Bennett, W. J. *The Index of Leading Cultural Indicators.* New York: Simon and Schuster, 1994.

Berenson, B. *The Passionate Sightseer.* New York: Simon and Schuster, 1960.

Berger, John. *Looking at Art.* New York: Pantheon Books, 1980.

Berleant, A. *The Aesthetic Field.* New York: Appleton-Century-Crofts, 1970.

Berleant, A. *Art and Engagement.* Philadelphia: Temple University Press, 1991.

Berlyne, D. E. *Aesthetics and Psychobiology.* New York: Appleton-Century-Crofts, 1971.

Berlyne, D. E. *Conflict, Arousal, and Curiosity.* New York: McGraw-Hill, 1960.

Berlyne, D. E. "Curiosity and Exploration." *Science* 153 (1966): 25–33.

Berlyne, D. E., ed. *Studies in the New Experimental Aesthetics.* Washington, D.C.: Hemisphere Publishing Corp, 1974.

Berry, W. *Structural Functions in Music.* Englewood Cliffs: Prentice-Hall, 1976.

Bessom, M. E., et al. *Teaching Music in Today's Secondary Schools.* New York: Holt, Rinehart & Winston, 1980.

Best, D. *Feeling and Reason in the Arts.* Boston: George Allen & Unwin, 1985.

Bettelheim, Bruno. *The Uses of Enchantment.* New York: Alfred A. Knopf, 1976.

Birkhoff, George. *Aesthetic Measure.* Cambridge: Harvard University Press, 1933.

Block, N., ed. *Imagery.* Cambridge, Mass.: MIT Press, 1981.

Briswell, Guy Thomas. *How People Look at Pictures: A Study of the Psychology of Perception in Art.* Chicago: University of Chicago Press, 1935.

Broadbent, D. *Perception and Communication.* New York: Pergamon Press, 1958.

Bruner, J. S. "On Perceptual Readiness." *Psychological Review* 64 (1957): 123–52.

Brunswik, E. *Perception and the Representative Design of Psychological Experiments.* Berkeley: University of California Press, 1956.

Butler, J. D. *Four Philosophies and Their Practice in Education and Religion.* New York: Harper & Brothers, 1957.

Campbell, D. *The Mozart Effect.* New York: Avon Books, 1997.

Carpenter, P. "Grundgestalt as Tonal Function." *Music Theory Spectrum* 5 (1983): 15–38.

Castro, J. G. *The Art and Life of Georgia O'Keeffe.* New York: Crown Publishers, 1985.

Cheney, S. *A New World History of Art.* New York: Holt, Rinehart and Winston, 1956.

Cleaver, D. G., and Eddins, J. M. *Art and Music: An Introduction.* New York: Harcourt Brace Jovanovich, 1977.

Cohen, J. E. "Information Theory and Music." *Behavioral Science* 7 (1962): 137–63.

Commons, M. L., ed. *Beyond Formal Operations.* New York: Praeger Publishers, 1984.

Commons, M. L., et al., eds. *Beyond Formal Operations: Late Adolescent and Adult Cognitive Development.* New York: Praeger Publishers, 1984.

Cone, E. T. "Musical Form and Music Performance Reconsidered." *Music Theory Spectrum* 3 (1981): 149–58.

Critchley, M., and Henson, R., eds. *Music and the Brain: Studies in the Neurology of Music.* Springfield, Ill.: Charles C. Thomas, 1977.

Cross, N. M., et al. *The Search for Personal Freedom.* Vol. 1. Dubuque, Iowa: Wm. C. Brown, 1972a.

Cross, N. M., et al. *The Search for Personal Freedom.* Vol. 2. Dubuque, Iowa: Wm. C. Brown, 1972b.

Crowder, R. G. "Imagery for Musical Timbre." *Journal of Experimental Psychology: Human Perception and Performance* 15 (1989): 472–78.

Crozier, W. R., and Chapman, A. J., eds. *Cognitive Processes in the Perception of Art.* Amsterdam: North-Holland Publishing Co., 1984.

Cuddy, L. L. "On Hearing Pattern in Melody." In *Psychology of Music.* Ed. D. Deutsch. New York: Academic Press, 1982. 3-10.

Cuddy, L. L., et al. "Melody Recognition: The Experimental Application of Musical Rules." *Canadian Journal of Psychology* 33 (1979): 148–157.

Danto, Arthur. *Transfigurations of the Commonplace.* Cambridge: Harvard University Press, 1981.

Davidson, R. J., and Schwartz, G. E. "The Influence of Musical Training on Patterns of

EEG Asymmetry During Musical and Non-Musical Self-Generation Tasks." *Psychophysiology* 14 (1977): 58–63.

DeBroder, G. W. "The Relationship of Improvement in Training of Musical Perception to Dimensions of the Personality." Ph.D. diss., University of Denver, 1970.

Demick, J., and Wapner, Seymour, eds. *Field Dependence-Independence: Bio-Psycho-Social Factors Across the Life Span.* Mahwah, N.J.: Erlbaum, Lawrence Associates, Inc., 1991.

Dennet, Daniel C. *Brainstorms: Philosophical Essays on Mind & Psychology.* Cambridge, Mass.: MIT Press, 1981.

Deutsch, D. "An Auditory Illusion." *Nature* 1251 (1974): 307–309.

Deutsch, D. "Memory and Attention in Music." In *Music and the Brain: Studies in the Neurology of Music.* Ed. M. Critchley and R. Henson. Springfield, Ill.: Charles C. Thomas, 1977. 95–127.

Deutsch, D. "Musical Recognition." *Psychological Review* 76 (1969): 300–307.

Deutsch, D. "Octave Generalization and the Consolidation of Melodic Information." *Canadian Journal of Psychology* 33 (1979): 201–5.

Deutsch, D., ed. *The Psychology of Music.* New York: Academic Press, 1982.

Dewey, John. *Reconstruction in Philosophy.* Boston: Beacon Press, 1957.

Dickie, George. "Evaluating Art." *British Journal of Aesthetics* 25 (winter 1985): 3–16.

Dissanayake, E. *What Is Art For?* Seattle: University of Washington Press, 1988.

Dorian, F. *The Musical Workshop.* London: Secker & Warburg, 1947.

Dowling, J. E. *Neurons and Networks: An Introduction to Neuroscience.* Cambridge: Harvard University Press, 1992.

Dowling, W. J. "Scale and Contour: Two Components of a Theory of Memory for Melodies." *Psychological Review* 85 (1978): 341–54.

Dowling, W. J., and Bartlett, J. C. "Assimilation of Brief Atonal Melodies to Tonal Prototypes: Asymmetrical Effects on Judgment." Paper presented at the meeting of the Psychonomic Society, Philadelphia, Pa., 1981.

Dudley, L., and Faricy, A. *The Humanities.* New York: McGraw-Hill, 1968.

Duncan-Johnson, C. C. "P300 Latency: A New Metric of Information Processing." *Psychophysiology* 18 (1981): 207–15.

Durant, W. *The Story of Philosophy: The Lives and Opinions of the Greater Philosophers.* New York: Simon and Schuster, 1953.

Eaton, M. *Art and Nonart: Reflections on an Orange Crate and a Moose Call.* New Brunswick, N.J.: Fairleigh Dickinson University Press, 1983.

Empson, J. *Human Brainwaves.* New York: Stockton Press, 1986.

Estes, W. K. *Models of Learning, Memory, and Choice.* New York: Praeger Publishers, 1982.

Farley, F. H., and Neperud, R. W. *The Foundations of Aesthetics, Art, and Art Education.* Westport, Conn.: Praeger Publishers, 1988.

Fiedler, Conrad. *On Judging Works of Visual Art.* Berkeley: University of California Press, 1949.

Finke, R. A., and Schmidt, M. J. "Orientation-Specific Color Aftereffects Following Imagination." *Journal of Experimental Psychology* 3 (1977): 599–606.

Fiske, H. E. "The Application of Stage Reduction Theory to Music Listening." *Psychology of Music* (Special Issue, 1982): 31–35.

Flavell, J. H. *The Developmental Psychology of Jean Piaget.* Princeton, N.J.: Van Nostrand, 1963.

Ford, J. M., and Hillyard, S. A. "Event-Related Potentials to Interruptions of Steady Rhythm." *Psychophysiology* 18 (1981): 322–30.

Franklin, M. B., and Kaplan, B., eds. *Development and the Arts: Critical Perspectives.* Hillsdale, N.J.: Lawrence Erlbaum Associates, 1994.

Fraser, J. T. "The Art of the Audible 'Now.'" *Music Theory Spectrum* 7 (1985): 181–84.

Gage, N. L. *Hard Gains in the Soft Sciences: The Case of Pedagogy.* Bloomington, Ind.: Center on Evaluation, Development and Research, 1985.

Gardner, H., ed. *The New Oxford Book of English Verse.* New York: Oxford University Press, 1972.

Gardner, J. W. *Excellence: Can We Be Equal and Excellent Too?* New York: W. W. Norton, 1984.

Gerdts, W. H. *American Impressionism.* New York: Abbeville Press, 1984.

Gibson, E. "Learning to Read." *Science* 148 (1965): 1066–72.

Gibson, E. *Principles of Perceptual Learning and Development.* New York: Appleton-Century-Crofts, 1969.

Gombrich, E. H. *Art and Illusion.* New York: Pantheon Books, 1960.

Goodman, N. *Languages of Art.* Indianapolis: Bobbs-Merrill Company, 1968.

Gordon, E. E. "Research Studies in Audiation." *Bulletin of the Council for Research in Music Education* 84 (1985): 34–50.

Greene, M. *Landscapes of Learning.* New York: Teachers College Press, Columbia University, 1978.

Grout, D. J., and Palisca, C. V. *A History of Western Music.* New York: W.W. Norton, 1988.

Hagberg, G. L. *Art as Language.* Ithaca, N.Y.: Cornell University Press, 1995.

Halpern, A. R. "Mental Scanning in Auditory Imagery for Songs." *Journal of Experimental Psychology: Learning, Memory, and Cognition* 14 (1988): 434–43.

Hanslick, E. *The Beautiful in Music.* Ed. Morris Weitz. Indianapolis: Bobbs-Merrill Company, 1957.

Harrison, F. L., and Westrup, Jack A., eds. *New College Encyclopedia of Music.* New York: W. W. Norton, 1960.

Harrison, T. *1910: The Emancipation of Dissonance.* Berkeley: University of California Press, 1996.

Hebb, D. O. "Concerning Imagery." *Psychological Review* 75 (1968): 466–75.

Hebb, D. O. *The Organization of Behavior: A Neuropsychological Theory.* New York: Wiley & Sons, 1949.

Hirsch, E. D. *Cultural Literacy: What Every American Needs to Know.* New York: Random House, 1988.

Hirsch, E. D. *Fairness and Core Knowledge.* Charlottesville: Core Knowledge Foundation, 1991.

Hood, J. D. "Psychological and Physiological Aspects of Hearing." In *Music and the Brain: Studies in the Neurology of Music.* Ed. M. Critchley and R. Henson. Springfield, Ill.: Charles C. Thomas, 1977. 4–46.

Hubbard, T. L., and Stoeckig, K. "Musical Imagery: Generation of Tones and Chords." *Journal of Experimental Psychology: Learning, Memory, and Cognition* 14 (1988): 656–67.

Hughes, R. *Culture of Complaint.* New York: Oxford University Press, 1993.

Hughes, R. *Nothing If Not Critical: Selected Essays on Art and Artists.* New York: Penguin Books, 1990.

Hume, David. *Hume Selections*. Ed. C. W. Hendel, Jr. New York: Charles Scribner's Sons, 1927.

Intons-Peterson, M. J., and McDaniel, M. A. "Symmetries and Asymmetries Between Imagery and Perception." *Imagery and Cognition* (1991): 47–76.

Janson, H. W., and Kerman, J. *A History of Art & Music*. Englewood Cliffs, N.J.: Prentice-Hall.

Jung, C. G. *Psychological Types*. Princeton, N.J.: Princeton University Press, 1971.

Kaelin, E. F. *An Aesthetics for Art Educators*. New York: Teachers College Press, 1989.

Kelley, E. C. *Education for What Is Real*. New York: Harper & Brothers, 1947.

Kellogg, R. T. "Long-Term Memory of Unattended Information." *Psychological Record* 35 (1985): 239–49.

Kivy, Peter. "Aesthetic Aspects and Aesthetic Qualities." *Journal of Philosophy* 65 (February 1968): 86–93.

Klein, M., et al. "People with Absolute Pitch Process Tones Without Producing a P300." *Science* 223 (1984): 1306–9.

Knobler, N. *The Visual Dialogue: An Introduction to the Appreciation of Art*. New York: Holt, Rinehart & Winston, 1980.

Koffka, Kurt. *The Growth of the Mind*. London: Kegan Paul, Ltd, 1924.

Koffka, Kurt. *Principles of Gestalt Psychology*. New York: Harcourt, Brace, 1935.

Korsmeyer, C. "On Distinguishing 'Aesthetic' and 'Artistic.'" *Journal of Aesthetic Education* 11 (1977): 45–57.

Kosslyn, S. M. *Ghosts in the Mind's Machine*. New York: W. W. Norton, 1983.

Kosslyn, S. M. *Image and Mind*. Cambridge: Harvard University Press, 1980.

Kosslyn, S. M., et. al. "The Medium and the Message in Mental Imagery: A Theory." *Psychological Review* 88 (1981): 46–66.

Krieger, M. *Arts on the Level: The Fall of the Elite Object*. Knoxville: University of Tennessee Press, 1981.

Kutas, M., and Hillyard, S. "Reading Senseless Sentences: Brain Potentials Reflect Semantic Incongruity." *Science* 207 (1980): 203–4.

Lang, P. H., ed. *Stravinsky: A New Appraisal of His Work*. New York: W. W. Norton, 1963.

Lang, P. J. "Cognition in Emotion: Concept and Action." *Emotions, Cognition, and Behavior*. Ed. Carroll E. Izard, Jerome Kagan, and Robert B. Zajone. New York: Cambridge University Press. 1984.

Lashley, K. S. "The Problem of Serial Order in Behavior." In *Cerebral Mechanisms in Behavior*. Ed. L. A. Jeffress. New York: John Wiley & Sons, 1951.

Leeuwenberg, E. "A Perceptual Coding Language for Visual and Auditory Patterns." *American Journal of Psychology* 84.3 (1971): 307–48.

Lehman, Paul R. *The National Standards: From Vision to Reality*. Reston, Va.: Music Educators National Conference, 1994.

Levin, H. *Accelerated Schools After Eight Years*. Palo Alto: Stanford University, 1994.

Levine, G., and Burke, C. J. *Mathematical Model Techniques for Learning Theories*. New York: Academic Press, 1972.

Lewis, C. "Tonal Focus in Atonal Music: Berg's Op. 5, No. 3." *Music Theory Spectrum* 3 (1981): 84–97.

Lindsay, P., and Norman, D. *Human Information Processing*. New York: Academic Press, 1977.

Long, N. H. "A Revision of the University of Oregon Music Discrimination Test." Ed.D. diss., Indiana University, 1965.

Matson, D. L. "Field Dependence—Independence in Children and Their Response to Musical Tasks Embodying Piaget's Principle of Conservation." Ph.D. diss., Ohio State University, 1978.

McKellar, P. *Imagination and Thinking*. New York: Basic Books, Inc., 1957.

Meyer, L. B. *Emotion and Meaning in Music*. Chicago: University of Chicago Press, 1956.

Meyer, L. B. *Music, the Arts, and Ideas: Patterns and Predictions in Twentieth Century Culture*. Chicago: University of Chicago Press, 1967.

Miller, R., and Colwell, R. "Aesthetic Response in Music: An Adaptation of the Perlmutter/Perkins Model." *A Model for Aesthetic Response in the Arts*. St. Louis: CEMREL, 1982.

Moles, A. *Information Theory and Esthetic Perception*. Urbana: University of Illinois Press, 1966.

Montague, W. P. *The Ways of Things*. New York: Prentice-Hall, 1940.

Mulder, G., et al. "Stage Analysis of the Reaction Process Using Brain-Evoked Potentials and Reaction Time." *Psychological Research* 46 (1984): 15–32.

Neimark, E. D., and Estes, W. K. *Stimulus Sampling Theory*. San Francisco: Holden-Day, 1967.

Nelson, D. J. "Trends in the Aesthetic Responses of Children to the Musical Experience." *Journal of Research in Music Education* 33.3 (1985): 193–203.

Nettl, B., et al. *Excursions in World Music*. Englewood Cliffs, N.J.: Prentice-Hall, 1992.

Norman, M. F. *Markov Processes and Learning Models*. New York: Academic Press, 1972.

O'Connor, N., and Hermelin, B. *Seeing and Hearing and Space and Time*. London: Academic Press, 1978.

Olson, I. *Developing Musical Awareness*. Minneapolis: Burgess Publishing Company, 1981.

Olson, I. "Measurement of Musical Awareness." *Bulletin of the Council for Research in Music Education* 77 (1984): 31–42.

Osgood, C. E., et al. *Measurement of Meaning*. Urbana: University of Illinois Press, 1957.

Paivio, A. *Imagery and Verbal Processes*. New York: Holt, Rinehart & Winston, 1971.

Paivio, A. *Mental Representations: A Dual Coding Approach*. New York: Oxford University Press, 1986.

Pflederer, M. "Conservation Laws Applied to the Development of Musical Intelligence." *Journal of Research in Music Education* 15 (1967): 215–23.

Piaget, Jean. *The Moral Judgment of the Child*. New York: Free Press, 1965.

Pick, A. D., et al. "Children's Perception of Certain Musical Properties: Scale and Contour." Unpublished Study. University of Minnesota, 1986.

Pierce, J. R. "Rate, Place, and Pitch with Tonebursts." *Music Perception* 7 (1990): 205–12.

Plomp, R. *Experiments in Tone Perception*. Eindhoven, The Netherlands: Institute for Perception, 1966.

Portnoy, J. *Music in the Life of Man*. New York: Holt, Rinehart & Winston, 1963.

Purcell, A. T. "The Aesthetic Experience and Mundane Reality." In *Cognitive Processes in the Perception of Art*. Ed. W. R. Crozier and A. J. Chapman. Amsterdam: North-Holland Publishing Co., 1984. 189-210.

Pylyshyn, Z. W. "The Imagery Debate: Analogue Media Versus Tacit Knowledge." *Psychological Review* 88 (1981): 16–45.

Rader, M., ed. *A Modern Book of Esthetics*. New York: Henry Holt and Co., 1952.

Read, H. *Icon and Idea*. New York: Schocken Books, 1965.

Read, H. *The Meaning of Art*. London: Pitman, 1951.

Restle, F. "A Theory of Discrimination Learning." *Psychological Review* 62 (1955): 11–19.

Richards, F. A. "Systematic, Metasystematic, and Cross-Paradigmatic Reasoning." In *Beyond Formal Operations*. Ed. M. L. Commons, et al. New York: Praeger Publishers, 1984. 92–119.

Rosenfeld, Anne. "The Roots of Individuality: Brain Waves and Perception: An NIMH Program Report." Washington, D.C.: U.S. Department of Health, Education and Welfare, 1976.

Rowell, L. "The Subconscious Language of Musical Time." *Music Theory Spectrum* 1 (1979): 96–106.

Ruskin, J. "The Novelty of Landscape." In *Modern Painters*. Vol. 3. London: Smith, Elder and Co., 1856. Reprinted in *Selections and Essays by John Ruskin*. New York: Charles Scribner's Sons, 1918.

Russ, S. W. *Affect and Creativity: The Role of Affect and Play in the Creative Process*. Hillsdale, N.J.: Lawrence Erlbaum Associates, 1993.

Sachs, C. *World History of the Dance*. New York: W. W. Norton, 1937.

Saldanha, E. "An Investigation into the Effects of Prolonged and Exacting Visual Work." Applied Psychology Unit Report No. 243. Cambridge, 1957.

Savile, A. *The Test of Time*. Oxford: The Clarendon Press, 1982.

Schoenberg, A. "Composition with Twelve Tones." In *Style and Idea: Selected Writings of Arnold Schoenberg*. Ed. Leonard Stein. New York: St. Martin's Press, 1975. 214-44.

Schuurmans, E., and Vandierendonck, A. "Recall as Communication: Effects of Frame Anticipation." *Psychological Research* 47 (1985): 119–24.

Schwadron, A. A. *Aesthetics: Dimensions for Music Education*. Washington, D.C.: Music Educators National Conference, 1967.

Schwarz, I. P., and Karel, L. C. *Teaching the Related Arts: A Guide to General Education in the Arts*. Kirksville, Mo.: Simpson Publishing Co., 1973.

Scruton, R. *The Aesthetics of Architecture*. Princeton, N.J.: Princeton University Press, 1979.

Segal, S. J., and Fusella, V. "Influence of Imaged Pictures and Sounds on Detection of Visual and Auditory Signals." *Journal of Experimental Psychology* 83 (1970): 458–64.

Serafine, M. L. "Cognition in Music." *Cognition* 14 (1983): 119–83.

Shannon, C. E., and Weaver, W. *The Mathematical Theory of Communication*. Urbana: University of Illinois Press, 1949.

Shepard, R. N. "Form, Formation, and Transformation of Internal Representations." *Information Processing and Cognition: Loyola Symposium*. Hillsdale, N.J.: Lawrence Erlbaum Associates, 1975.

Sloboda, J. A. "Perception of Contour in Music Reading." *Perception* 7 (1978): 323–31.

Smith, R. A. *The Sense of Art: A Study in Aesthetic Education*. New York: Routledge, 1989.

Smith, R. A., ed. *Aesthetics and Problems of Education*. Urbana: University of Illinois Press, 1971.

Southern, E., ed. *Readings in Black American Music*. New York: W. W. Norton, 1971.

Sparshott, F. E. "The Unity of Aesthetic Education." In *Aesthetics and Problems of Education*. Ed. R. A. Smith. Urbana: University of Illinois Press, 1971. 243–57.

Stahl, G. "Sibley's 'Aesthetic Concepts': An Ontological Mistake." *Journal of Aesthetics and Art Criticism* 29 (1971): 385–90.

Sternberg, R. J. "Higher-Order Reasoning in Postformal Operational Thought." In *Beyond Formal Operations*. Ed. M. L. Commons. New York: Praeger Publishers, 1984. 74–90.

Stolnitz, J. *Aesthetics and Philosophy of Art Criticism: A Critical Introduction*. Boston: Houghton Mifflin Co., 1960.

Suppes, P., and Ginsberg, R. "Experimental Studies of Mathematical Concept Formation in Young Children." *Science Education* 46 (1962): 230–40.

Tanner, P., and Gerow, M. *A Study of Jazz*. Dubuque, Iowa: Wm. C. Brown, 1964.

Thorndike, R. L. *Intelligence as Information Processing: The Mind and the Computer*. Bloomington, Ind.: Phi Delta Kappa, 1984.

Tucker, W. T. "Experiments in Aesthetic Communications." Ph.D. diss., University of Illinois, 1955.

Tye, Michael. *The Imagery Debate*. Cambridge, Mass.: The MIT Press, 1991.

Ullman, S. "Visual Routines." *Cognition* 18 (1984): 97–159.

Underwood, G. *Attention and Memory*. Oxford: Pergamon Press, 1976.

Vernon, M. D. *A Further Study of Visual Perception*. Cambridge: Cambridge University Press, 1954.

Veron, E. *Aesthetics*. Trans. W. H. Armstrong. London: Chapman & Hall, 1879.

Vivas, Eliseo. *The Artistic Transaction*. Columbus: Ohio State University Press, 1963.

Vyverberg, H. *The Living Tradition: Art, Music, and Ideas in the Western World*. New York: Harcourt Brace Jovanovich, 1978.

Wellmer, A. *The Persistence of Modernity*. Cambridge, Mass.: The MIT Press, 1991.

Wilson, A. V. *Design for Understanding Music*. Evanston, Ill.: Summy-Birchard, 1966.

Wilson, K. V. *From Associations to Structure*. Amsterdam: North-Holland Publishing Co., 1980.

Wilton, A. *Turner and the Sublime*. Chicago: University of Chicago Press, 1980.

Witkin, H. A. *Personality through Perception*. New York: Harper, 1954.

Witkin, H. A., et al. *A Manual for the Embedded Figures Tests*. Palo Alto, Calif.: Consulting Psychologists Press, 1971.

Wittgenstein, L. "Lowry and the Industrial North." In *About Looking*. Ed. Kenneth Clark. New York: Pantheon Books, 1980.

Wittgenstein, L. *Philosophical Investigations*. New York: Macmillan, 1953.

Wold, M., et al. *An Introduction to Music and Art in the Western World*. Dubuque, Iowa: Wm. C. Brown, 1987.

Ziff, P. "Reasons in Art Criticism." In *Philosophy and Education*. Ed. Israel Scheffler. Boston, 1958. 219–36.

Index

About the Author

IVAN OLSON was Visiting Professor at the School of Education, University of North Carolina at Chapel Hill.